ATLAS
of
EXTRATERRESTRIAL ZONES

BRUNO FULIGNI

Illustrations by François Moreno

ATLAS
of
EXTRATERRESTRIAL
ZONES

SCHIFFER
PUBLISHING

4880 Lower Valley Road · Atglen, PA 19310

Originally published as *L'Atlas des zones extraterrestres*, ©2017 Flammarion, Paris
Translated from the French by Rebecca DeWald.

Library of Congress Control Number: 2022944221

Type set in Monopoly/Ailerons

ISBN: 978-0-7643-6593-5
Printed in Portugal

Published by Schiffer Publishing, Ltd.
4880 Lower Valley Road
Atglen, PA 19310
Phone: (610) 593-1777; Fax: (610) 593-2002
Email: Info@schifferbooks.com
Web: www.schifferbooks.com

For our complete selection of fine books on this and related subjects, please visit our website at www.schifferbooks.com. You may also write for a free catalog.

Schiffer Publishing's titles are available at special discounts for bulk purchases for sales promotions or premiums. Special editions, including personalized covers, corporate imprints, and excerpts, can be created in large quantities for special needs. For more information, contact the publisher.

We are always looking for people to write books on new and related subjects. If you have an idea for a book, please contact us at proposals@schifferbooks.com.

It is as absurd to conceive of a wheat field with a single stem
as it is to imagine just a single world in the vast universe.

—METRODORUS, *Epicurean philosopher*
of the third century BCE

CONTENTS

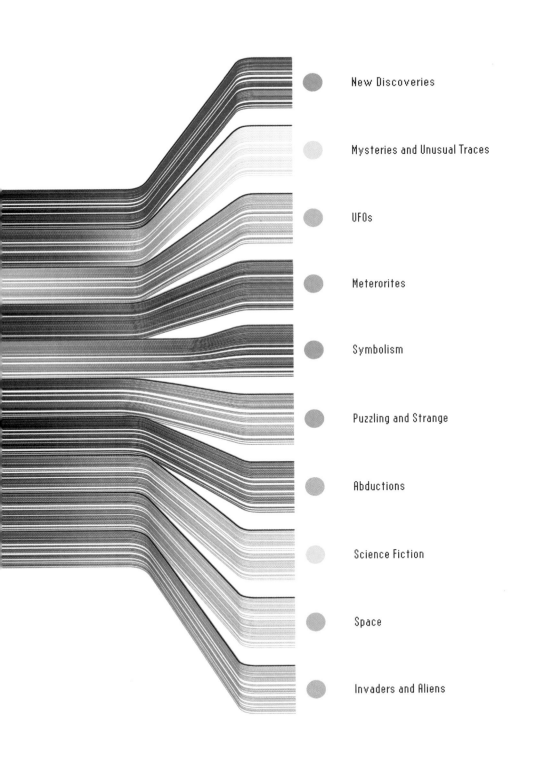

New Discoveries

Mysteries and Unusual Traces

UFOs

Meterorites

Symbolism

Puzzling and Strange

Abductions

Science Fiction

Space

Invaders and Aliens

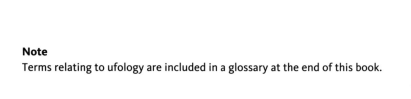

Note

Terms relating to ufology are included in a glossary at the end of this book.

INTRODUCTION

Where is the best place to meet benevolent aliens? How do we communicate with intelligent interstellar life forms, socialize with Grays, and avoid bloodthirsty Reptilians? Can you learn Martian? And where have accounts by "contactees" and "abductees" been saved that have accumulated over the past seventy years?

Mythomaniacs, impostors, and gurus abound in the world of ufology, yet governments have also taken some of the reported and hard-to-explain signals more seriously: thanks to the data collected by the military and scientists, intelligence services, and international organizations, we are able to map out this phenomenon today.

Locations of sightings, hidden bases, and secret embassies, and traces of thousand-year-old passages, from the UFO port of Arès to the underground center of Area 51, from the crash at Roswell to setting up the SETI program: this atlas lists, for the first time, the meeting points between earthlings and EBE—these mysterious extraterrestrial biological entities.

Of course, you can smirk at these undertakings, but it is also worth remembering that it is through pondering the stars that humankind first began to think. Similarly, the observation of spatial phenomena is linked to the awakening of abstract thought, and while it may not be possible for everyone to meet the alien of their dreams or to beget a "cosmic child," the act of reflection itself makes us grow and leads us to question our position at the center of the universe.

The Greek philosopher Epicurus considered the infinity of the universe as early as the third century BCE, concluding in almost statistical terms: "There is an infinite number of worlds, some like this world, others unlike it," he wrote in his *Letter to Herodotus.*

Already rejected by Aristotle, the champion of anthropocentrism, this notion became thoroughly heretical in the Christian world, and it took all the courage of a thinker such as Bernard le Bovier de Fontenelle to rebut it. His refutation took the form of learned and gallant dalliances with a witty Marchioness, his *Conversations on the Plurality of Worlds.*

"Enormous bodies, extending their white wings to the blast, come sailing on the ocean with fearful rapidity, and discharging fire on every side: these tremendous machines cast on their shore men covered with iron; guiding with facility the monsters that carry them, and darting thunderbolts from their hands to destroy all who attempt to resist them. Whence come these awful beastings? Who hath given them power to ride on the waters and to wield the thunder of heaven? Are they children of the sun? Assuredly they are not men!" (translated by Miss Elizabeth Gunning, 1803). This is not taken from a science fiction novel (before the term was even coined), but it is how Fontenelle summed up, in 1686, "a spectacle new and astonishing" that Native Americans encountered as they watched the conquistadores disembark. And, by analogy, he makes the leap to suggest that one day, the inhabitants of another earth, which we don't yet know exists, may unexpectedly surprise us here, just like the First Nations of the Americas were surprised since they did not know of the existence of Europe.

"Oh! How glad I should be," exclaimed the Marchioness, "for a shipwreck to cast a good number of them on the earth; we might then examine them at our leisure." The frivolous Marchioness somehow anticipated Roswell. But her cautious interlocutor does not hesitate to reply: "If they were clever enough to navigate the surface of our atmosphere and, from a curiosity to examine us, should be tempted to draw us up like fishes, would that please you?" "Why not?" answered she, laughing. "I would voluntarily put myself in their nets, just for the pleasure of seeing the fishers."

A map of portals that open up between the worlds, a geography of strange events that covers the whole planet earth, demonstrating how widespread the phenomenon is.

But it is not until the end of World War II that these old philosophical assumptions would be backed up by experience: from 1944 onward, Air Force pilots noticed foo fighters or small fireballs whizzing around their aircraft. On June 24, 1947, the first sighting of "flying saucers" occurred over Mount Rainier in the United States, accompanied by several eyewitness accounts and followed by noticeable "waves" of sightings in 1954 and 1976.

Admittedly, the pyramids of Egypt and other ancient monuments have been interpreted as the remains of societies that once came into contact with alien civilizations. However, these explanations were not suggested until after these unusual postwar years and only retroactively applied to thousands of recorded observations that had much in common with the fears of and experiments conducted during the Cold War. The famous psychologist Carl Gustav Jung wrote about a "visionary rumor" and was so worried about the phenomenon of flying saucers that he published an essay on the subject in 1961, titled *Flying Saucers: A Modern Myth of Things Seen in the Sky*. "We have here a golden opportunity of seeing how a legend is formed, and how in a difficult and dark time for humanity a miraculous tale grows up," he analyzes, interpreting the witnesses' and ufologists' accounts by the "intervention by extra-terrestrial 'heavenly' powers" (translated by R. F. C. Hull).

Is this the opposite effect of nuclear weapons, their use having attracted rather than deterred observers and exterminators from other planets? Or is it modern humans' bad conscience who, frightened by our own power of destruction, feel we are constricted by Earth and are seeking new horizons? Are these simply fleeting observations of Cold War planes and drone tests that would no longer impress anyone today, or the first real manifestations of those other worlds that humans have always wished existed?

Celestial signs have lent themselves naturally to the most-diverse interpretations, so an atlas has of yore been the best way to objectively chart them. Not in the sense of celestial cartography, for that matter, but an atlas of those places on Earth where contacts, abductions, and other encounters of the third kind have been recorded: a map of portals that open up between the worlds, a geography of strange events that covers the whole planet Earth, demonstrating how widespread the phenomenon is.

Amateur ufologists will find in this atlas a travel guide, conspiracy theorists a practical manual for alien invasions, and "pelicanists" or skeptics will discover the new frontier of utopic thought. As for potential extraterrestrial readers, we hope you are lenient with us.

Inverness

Tory Island

Leipzig

London

Brussels

Morsbach

Marliens

Geneva

Migné-Auxances

Val Camonica

Arès

Chabeuil

Fátima

EUROPE

Moscow

46° 0' 30" N, 10° 20' 50" E

PREHISTORIC COSMONAUTS

VAL CAMONICA (ITALY)

Were our ancestors aliens? This is how the thesis about "ancient astronauts" can be summarized, tracing the source of our civilization back to visitors to planet Earth arriving from faraway places. Did they create life and inspire all creation myths of human religions? Or did they merely trigger the evolution of lowly primates by bringing them the means of technical progress unthinkable to them?

Proving this bold reinterpretation of the tumultuous history of humankind requires a return to prehistoric traces of encounters of the third kind—which is not easy. It is nevertheless what the Swiss researcher Erich von Däniken attempted to do, reinterpreting the world's major sites.

The most fascinating clue is located in Italy, in the Alpine reliefs of the province of Brescia. This is where the extraordinary site of Val Camonica is, listed as a World Heritage site thanks to its rock drawings, the oldest of which date back to the eighth millennium BCE. These close to 140,000 petroglyphs feature animals, symbols, and people, as well as some more mysterious representations, among them a famous scene depicting two levitating spacemen: two men facing each other, their heads clearly covered by something that looks like a space helmet! One is brandishing a weapon, the other

a strange tool that could be interpreted as a navigational instrument. These characters, drawn with chalk upon a dark backdrop, strangely protrude from the rock as if they were cruising through space. The anonymous Mesolithic artist who traced these extraordinary silhouettes, thereby colliding prehistory and space exploration, could not have guessed that these would provide the cover for numerous books on ufology, including the 1990 edition of Däniken's *Chariots of the Gods*, first published in 1968.

> Two levitating spacemen: two men facing each other, their heads clearly covered by something that looks like a space helmet!

Similar depictions can be visited not far from here, across the French border, in the Vallée des Merveilles: the Wonder Valley. In sixteenth-century Nice, and more recently in Valensole and Blausasc, numerous eyewitness accounts have described heavy UFO traffic, as if the great Alpine Piedmont region, from Digne to San Marino, remained a popular destination for EBE: extraterrestrial biological entities.

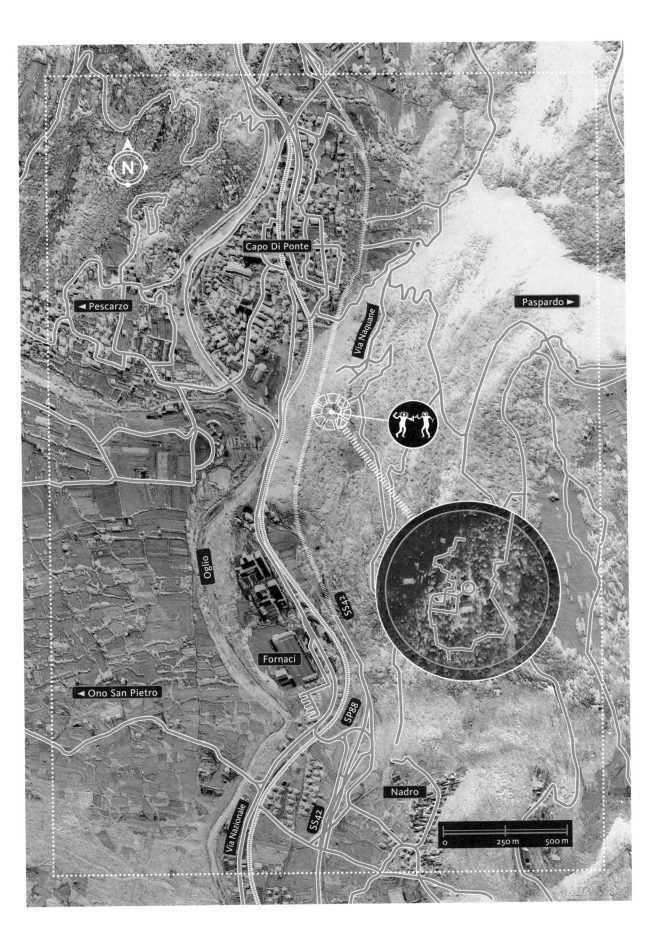

Capo Di Ponte

◄ Pescarzo

Paspardo ►

Via Naquane

Oglio

SS42

Fornaci

◄ Ono San Pietro

SP88

Nadro

Via Nazionale

SS42

0   250 m   500 m

57° 28' 57" N, 4° 14' 13" W

THE VITRIFIED FORT OF CRAIG PHADRIG

INVERNESS (SCOTLAND)

Loch Ness is certainly not the only one of Scotland's mysteries: towering at an altitude of 564 feet (172 meters), the old fort of Craig Phadrig attracts curious visitors because of its bizarre great walls, which are more than 3 feet (1 meter) thick and enclose an area of 246 by 75 feet (70 by 25 meters). A basic fortress that possibly dates as far back as the Iron Age, though it was destroyed shortly after its construction.

> Could it be that a swarm of UFOs appeared in time immemorial, ravaging human-made fortresses with their powerful rays?

The fortress's peculiarity is the very materials of its walls: the stone has become vitrified as if it had been exposed to extreme temperatures above 1,832 degrees Fahrenheit (1,000 degrees Celsius). It is simply unimaginable that humans could have produced such intense heat, or indeed why, since a vitrified wall is more fragile than a stone wall, reducing its defensive properties.

Or was it an attack? But what kind of army could have scorched the besieged citadel like that, without highly advanced technology? Those are the trains of thought of ufologists in an attempt to explain the riddle of vitrified forts.

While Craig Phadrig may be the most emblematic example of vitrified forts or walls, there are others like it elsewhere in Scotland and Ireland, as well as in France and central Europe. Could it be that a swarm of UFOs appeared in time immemorial, ravaging human-made fortresses with their powerful rays? This is a bold proposition, to say the least, but there is no other explanation to account for the glassy, translucent walls that hide, in their eternal silence, the mystery of Craig Phadrig.

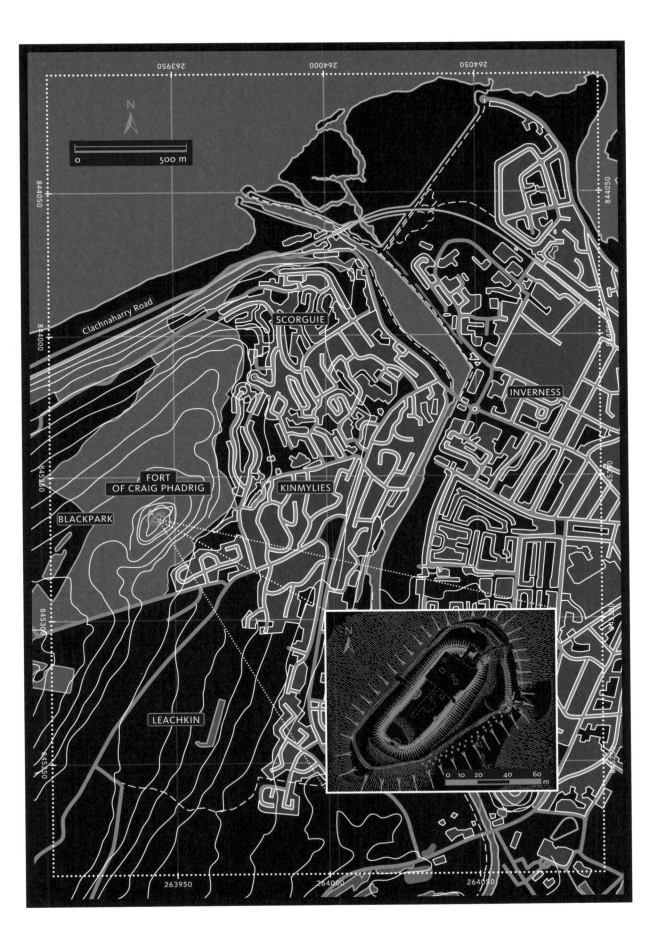

N

0   500 m

Clachnaharry Road

SCORGUIE

INVERNESS

FORT
OF CRAIG PHADRIG

KINMYLIES

BLACKPARK

LEACHKIN

263950

264000

264050

263950

264000

264050

844050

844000

843350

843300

843350

844050

844000

843350

843300

N

0 10 20   40   60
m

55° 15' 55" N, 8° 13' 49" W

THE GLASS TOWER OF THE FOMORIANS

TORY ISLAND (IRELAND)

Tory Island—Oileán Thoraigh in Gaelic—is in Northern Ireland. It has only two hundred inhabitants and a single pub, yet it has a customary king who greets visitors, and now also tourists, as they get off their boats.

> Their kingdom had a formidable weapon: a glass tower, from which the giant Balor projected a lethal ray whenever he opened his seven eyelids.

This good-humored and eccentric ruler, elected spokesperson by his people, also embodies the island's deep-seated rebellious spirit, already mentioned in Ireland's oldest chronicles. These also make mention of an otherwise fierce monarch, the dreaded Conand, King of the Fomorians, who chose Tory Island as the center of his dominion. His people were nothing like humans: the Fomorians were described as being formed of "one arm, one leg, and one eye" and were sometimes depicted in the shape of baboon-like creatures. Their kingdom had a formidable weapon: a glass tower, from which the giant Balor projected a lethal ray whenever he opened his seven eyelids. Was this a living creature or a killing machine? The Fomorians came from a distant world, the "Islands in the North of the World," of which nothing is known. That is why the fable allows for the most bizarre of ufological interpretations.

Nowadays, Tory Island, with its cliffs and its heaps of craggy loose stones, is nothing but a semiwild day-trip destination. Its lighthouse, however, slicing the night with its beam, oddly recalls the flashing tower of the former Fomorians—and perhaps a lost ufonaut may dock here one day.

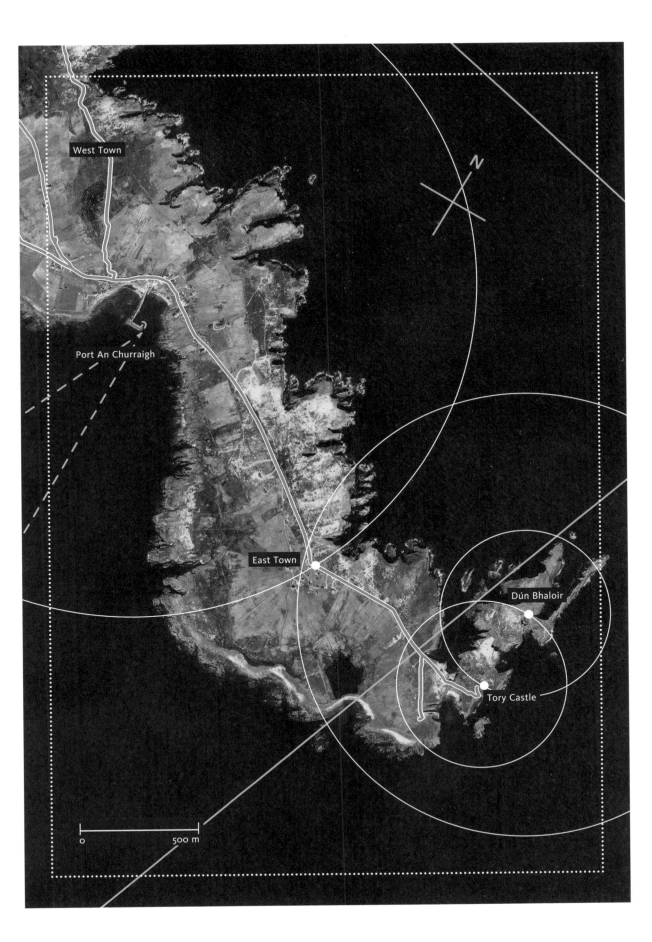

West Town

Port An Churraigh

East Town

Dún Bhaloir

Tory Castle

N

0   500 m

51° 20' 19" N, 12° 22' 43" E

THE AMPHITHEATER OF LIGHT

LEIPZIG (GERMANY)

*I*n September 1768, a stagecoach stopped briefly on its way to Leipzig. Travelers got out to stretch their legs, and one of them, nineteen years of age, went off for a short walk. At the end of the trail, he suddenly had a breathtaking vision: "I saw a sort of amphitheater, wonderfully illuminated," he summarized in his autobiography *Poetry and Truth* (translated by John Oxenford and A. J. W. Morrison).

For this young man was Johann Wolfgang von Goethe: still a student at the time of his observation, he would go on to become the great writer of German Romanticism. At that moment, however, he was just like a moth hypnotized by a beam of light: "In a funnel-shaped space there were innumerable little lights gleaming," he added, "and they shone so brilliantly that the eye was dazzled. But what stiff more confused the sight was that they did not keep still but jumped about here and there, as well as downward from above as vice versa, and in every direction. The most of them, however, remained stationary and beamed on."

The stagecoach was about to leave, and the disgruntled passengers were looking for the haughty young man who had so imprudently left the group. "It was only with the greatest reluctance that I suffered myself to be called away from this spectacle, which I could have

wished to examine more closely," Goethe recalls. "On interrogating the postillion, he indeed knew nothing about such a phenomenon."

This man of the Enlightenment wanted to find out more. He went on to live until the age of eighty-two and would devote his existence to knowledge. A writer, a poet, but also a geologist, a physicist, and a freemason of the highest rank, this lover of knowledge left behind a curious *Theory of Colors*, in which he questions the nature of chromaticism and humankind's visual perception.

> In a funnel-shaped space there were innumerable little lights gleaming.

Was Goethe a "contactee"? Did his curiosity lead him quite naturally to this hub of light, or was it this experience of radiating light that made him the great mind we know today? "The genius takes the good where he finds it," he wrote. And this encounter with a spacecraft that came from another world allows for a peculiar interpretation of this intellectual self-portrait: "Who am I? What did I create? Everything that I have seen, heard, and observed I have collected and exploited. . . . My work is the work of a collective being that bears the name of Goethe."

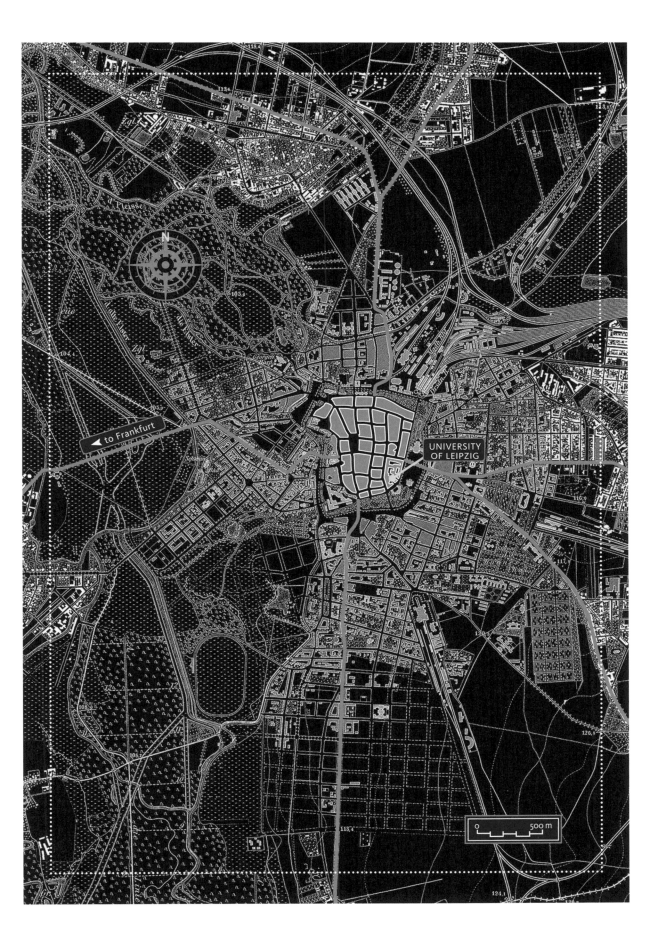

46° 37' 18" N, 0° 18' 25" E

THE CELESTIAL CROSS OF MIGNÉ

MIGNÉ-AUXANCES (FRANCE)

On December 17, 1826, the inhabitants of Migné, a small town north of the French town of Poitiers, gathered in the open air to erect a cross. The congregation was listening piously to their priest's sermon when they suddenly witnessed a miracle: a cross appeared in the sky, lying on its side, hovering immobile above their church.

"Monseigneur," wrote the parish priest of Migné to the bishop, together with two further priests, and about forty witnesses, "it appeared in the lower region of the air, above the small square located in front of the main portal of the church, a radiant cross raised above the ground by about 100 feet, allowing us to assess the length of the cross, which seemed to be 80 feet: its proportions were very regular, and its contours, which could be identified with the utmost clarity, stood out clearly from the cloudless sky, which, however, had begun to darken, since it was almost five o'clock in the evening. This cross, silver in color, was placed horizontally in the direction of the church, with its descending arm elevated and its upper beam resting; its color was the same throughout the length of it, and it remained unchanged for about half an hour; eventually, with the procession retiring to the church, the cross disappeared."

That very moment, all believers had thrown themselves down on their knees, their hands raised to heaven and singing with fervor the hymn "Vive Jésus, vive sa Croix" ("Long live Jesus, long live his Cross")! "It is impossible to fathom, Monseigneur, the sudden religious fervor that captured the spectators at the appearance of this cross," insists the parish priest of Migné.

Was it a miracle, a collective hallucination? In the context of the Bourbon Restoration in France, the apparition of Migné incited lively religious debates between supporters of the church and freethinkers. Nowadays, ufologists have become interested in it again, considering that it may not have been the apparition of a Catholic cross lying on its side but standing up—that is, they assume a spaceship, or a light signal, might have appeared above the congregation.

> They suddenly witnessed a miracle: a cross appeared in the sky, lying on its side, hovering immobile above their church.

The bishop of Poitiers, Monseigneur Bouillé, defended the Christian nature of this miracle. He had the church expanded in the shape of a cross and reoriented to face west, in the direction of the miraculous appearance; inside, a large copper cross was attached to the arch of the transept.

The tombstone of Bishop Bouillé in the Cathedral of Poitiers also recounts the scene of the hovering cross, as does the altar of St. Radegonde, patron saint of Poitiers, in the Sacré-Coeur basilica in Montmartre, Paris.

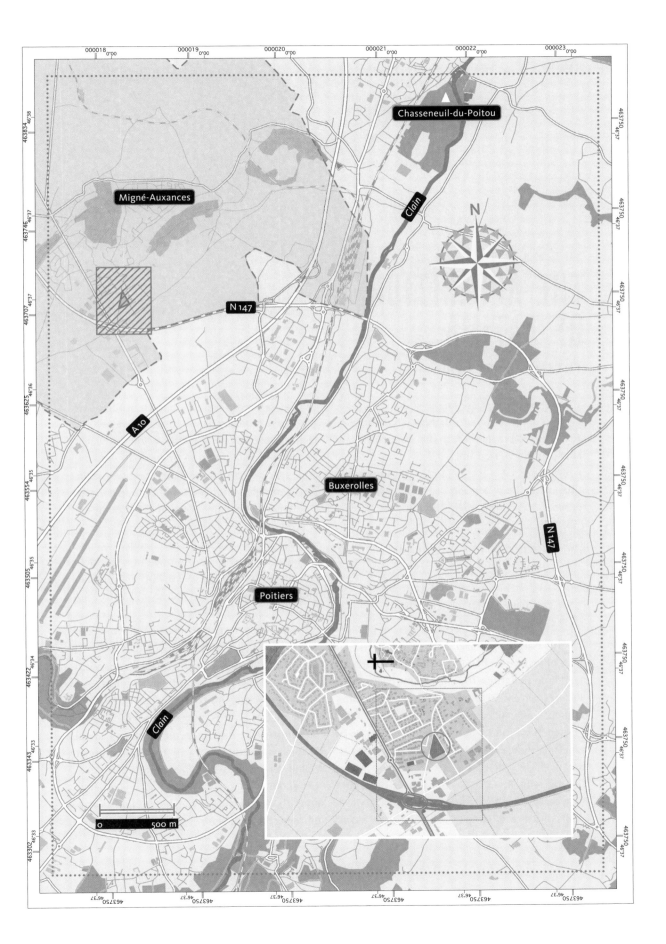

39° 37' 0" N, 8° 39' 7" W

THE APPARITIONS OF FÁTIMA

FÁTIMA (PORTUGAL)

After the cross of Migné, it would be easy enough to relate all Christian miracles to ufology, including the apparitions of Mary, Mother of God, of La Salette in 1851, and of Lourdes in 1862. . . . Yet, ufologists hardly ever do this—with the exception of the apparitions of Fátima, which seem to be different.

> Suddenly, many people raised their arms to point at a luminous ball in the sky, coming from the Orient.

In Lourdes, the Virgin Mary revealed herself to a young girl, Bernadette Soubirous—that is, to her alone. In Fátima, the apparitions occurred in 1917 over several months, before an ever-growing audience, and, more importantly, after the initial Marian apparition described by three shepherd children, they changed: from a lightning bolt to an angel and a fireball.

On August 13, 1917, thousands of people awaited a new apparition of the Virgin Mary, while the three children were kept away by a local civil servant who feared a breach of the peace. They saw "a bright globe turning on itself," as Manuel Pedro Masto, one of the countless eyewitnesses, recalls—he swore under oath when an ecclesiastical inquiry took place to give a ruling on the miraculous character of the apparitions.

A month later, the crowd doubled again, and two investigative priests were on the scene to witness the incredible event: "Suddenly, many people raised their arms to point at a luminous ball in the sky, coming from the Orient" and then moving toward the sun, "calmly but with some speed, before disappearing."

For believers, the "Miracle of the Sun" had occurred, whereby the sun had spun on itself, taking on the appearance of a silver disc. The former shepherd's children, Jacinta and Francisco Marto, joined in 2005 by their friend Lúcia de Los Santos, now rest in peace under the impressive Sanctuary of Our Lady of the Rosary, whose 213-foot-tall (65 meter) central bell tower seems to launch an attack on the sky. The small Portuguese town is now a very popular Catholic pilgrimage site, but ufologists have more heretical beliefs.

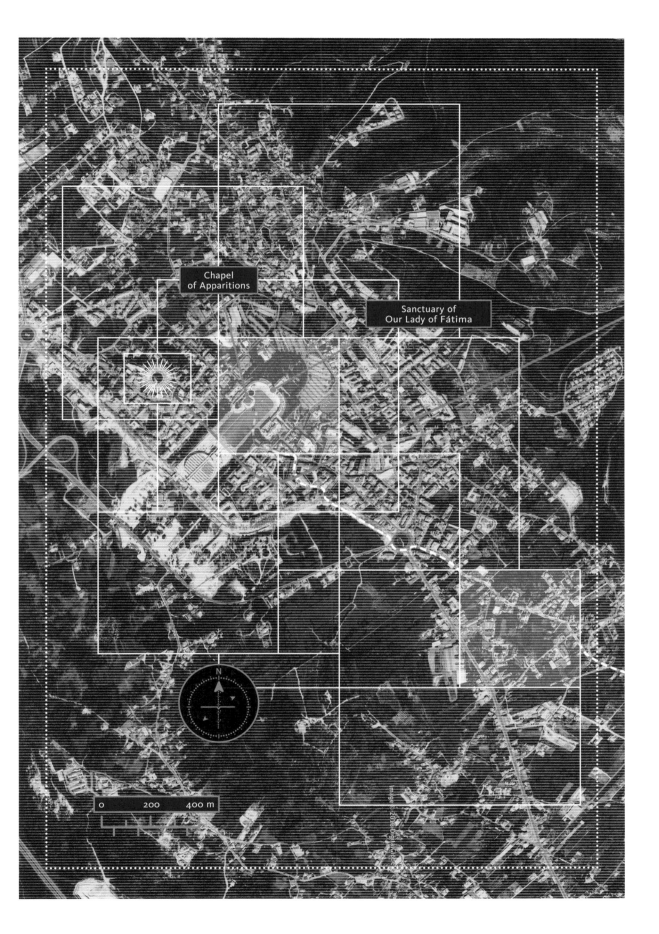

Chapel
of Apparitions

Sanctuary of
Our Lady of Fátima

N

0   200   400 m

51° 30' 26" N, 0° 7' 39" W

THE CALL OF THE XIPÉHUZ

LONDON (UNITED KINGDOM)

In London, on a cold day in 1883, a young Joseph-Henri Boex walked over one of the bridges crossing the river Thames. In the triumphant days of industrialism, Britain's capital was being inundated by fog, a thick layer that mixed the naturally occurring mist with the noxious fumes from factories and workshops. Boex, a twenty-seven-year-old Belgian dreamer, was pondering his literary future. He stopped on the parapet for an instant and suddenly made out a surprising light piercing the grayness. "At first, it was a large circle of bluish cones, translucent, with their apex pointing upward, each of about half the size of a man. A few bright stripes, some dark rings were dotted across their surface; each of them had a dazzling star at their base

"Farther away, and just as strange, there were vertically settled rocks, quite similar to birch bark and patterned with multicolored ellipses. There were also almost cylindrical Shapes here and there, varied in kind, some thin and tall, others short and squat, all of a bronze color with green dots, and all having, like the rocks, that characteristic point of light."

This phantasmagoria gave him vertigo. Could these be nonorganic living beings who had come from who knows where? A century earlier, Casanova had already witnessed such a luminescent phenomenon, "a pyramidal flame the height of a cubit," appearing without any explanation from another world and following him an entire night long somewhere near Rome. Several witnesses after him went on to describe animated sticks, so-called "rods," without any evidence of them being extraterrestrials, but which nevertheless are beyond any logical zoological classification. Boex, for his part, called the "Shapes" he perceived "Xipéhuz," a mysterious onomatopoeia that seems to evoke the deaf humming sound emanating from these translucent and geometric people.

> Could such luminescent entities be intelligent, and enter into conflict with humans?

Could such luminescent entities be intelligent, enter into conflict with humans, and try to take over our planet? "Whatever the nature of these Shapes, they acted like beings, not like the elements, and, like beings, their pace varied and differed, clearly choosing their victims," wrote Boex in *The Xipéhuz*, a novella he published in 1887 with his brother, under the pseudonym of J.-H. Rosny. He would, later on, become known as a genius novelist under the nom de plume of Rosny aîné. Transposing his London fulguration to ancient Mesopotamia, the young visionary had invented a new literary genre: science fiction.

Euston

Clerkenwell

Covent
Garden

City

Thames

St. James

London
Bridge

Pimlico

Camberwell

0   500 m   1 km

46° 12' 15" N, 6° 8' 35" E

THE MARTIAN LANGUAGE SCHOOL

GENEVA (SWITZERLAND)

From the very beginning, Miss Smith saw a bright glow in the distance and at a great height. Then she experienced a swaying motion that made her feel nauseated; after that, it seemed to her as if her head were empty and that she had ceased to have a body," according to the minutes of the event. Did she go into orbit, or was she abducted? Not at all: this space journey took place entirely in her mind, at a pedestal table where a small group of Spiritualists had entered into a state of trance.

It is November 25, 1894, in Geneva, and all those present are preparing to converse with the dead, as they usually do, under the guidance of their medium, Hélène Smith. But the calling of the spirits takes a radically different turn: "Miss Smith, who had felt unwell, was now better and made out three huge globes, one of which was very beautiful. 'What am I walking on?' she asked. And the people around the table replied: 'On the lands of Mars.'"

Soon, Smith began to speak in Martian, to even write it: she wrote down the alphabet and taught it to her circle of insiders. Esénale, a guide who accompanied her on her spiritual journey, taught her the basics until she became bilingual and wrote directly in the language of the red planet: she jotted down "Métiche" for "sir" and "Médache" for "lady," and "miss" was "Méganiche." "I Men danda ana" translates as "Quiet now, my friend!" And soon enough, the Martian speakers of Geneva were capable of articulating sentences as complex as "Véchêsi tésée polluni avè métiche é vi ti bounié, seïmiré ni triné," which means "Now this question, old man; it is for thee to seek, to understand and speak."

Hélène Smith's interplanetary mediumship attracted the attention of the Spiritualist doctor Théodore Flournoy, who devoted a book to her with the incredible title *From India to the Planet Mars*. The medium, whose real name was Catherine-Elise Müller, was a Swiss national with a Hungarian father, born in Martigny in 1861. A simple employee in a trading firm, she had made a name for herself as a reliable medium over the years. She had already invented a Sanskrit-inspired language she used in a "Hindu novel" dictated to her by voices from the afterlife. Later, Marie Antoinette inspired her to write frenzied letters in a "royal cycle" that were completely fictionalized. In short, Flournoy saw in her nothing more than a case of "sleepwalking with glossolalia," similar to plain dementia. In particular, Hélène Smith's Martian combined all the grammatical structures of French with a few loan words from her paternal Hungarian . . .

> She jotted down "*Métiche*" for "sir," and "*Médache*" for "lady," and "miss" was "*Méganiche*." "*I Men danda ana*" translates as "Quiet now, my friend!"

A wealthy, and more trusting, American woman paid Hélène Smith an allowance up until her death in 1929, so she could devote herself to spiritual exchanges with Mars. Toward the end of her life, she received messages in "Ultramartian," the vernacular of a secondary planet whose writing, in the form of strange figures in broken lines, would go on to dazzle the surrealists.

LAC DE GENEVE

Avenue Théodore-Flournoy

University of Geneva

50° 49' 52" N, 4° 23' 37" E

THE CAPITAL OF MARXIST UFOLOGY

BRUSSELS (BELGIUM)

Brussels is not only the capital of Belgium and the location of the European Commission: at 62, Rue des Cultivateurs, modest premises are home to the permanent services of the International Posadist, the guardian of the great dream of intergalactic emancipation.

Although little known, posadism is not an unusual ideology. This worldview is the brainchild of Juan Posadas, the moniker or revolutionary nickname of Argentine Trotskyist Homero Rómulo Cristalli Frasnelli. Born in 1912, the trade unionist founded the Revolutionary Workers Party in his home country in 1947, before repressive measures forced him to flee to Europe. He died on May 14, 1981, in Rome, after having made a name for himself as the father of Marxist ufology thanks to his major text, published in 1968: *Flying Saucers, the Process of Matter and Energy, Science and Socialism.*

"The existence of flying saucers and of beings coming to Earth is a phenomenon admissible by the dialectical conception of history," Posadas wrote. He never claimed to have encountered extraterrestrials or seen UFOs himself, but he posited a simple hypothesis that he resolved by applying Marxist theory with strict logic.

He concluded that "these beings, if they exist, possess a social organization superior to our own," which means that they have overcome class struggle, "since their appearance is not bellicose or aggressive," in contrast with bourgeois colonizers or the oppressors of the proletariat.

> "The existence of flying saucers and of beings coming to Earth is a phenomenon admissible by the dialectical conception of history."

From this, he derived the notion of the emancipation of humankind that supported workers who had originated from extraterrestrial civilizations in a spirit of solidarity: "All the witnesses confirm having seen no aggressive attitude. They all say that they felt no fear and that their curiosity was aroused.... Such behavior testifies to a superior form of organization by nonaggressive beings that do not need to kill in order to live and have simply come to observe.

"One can admit to the existence of such beings beyond the fancifulness in the reports, stories, observations, and statements. If they

exist, we must call on them to intervene and help solve the problems on Earth! They have come to study the people of the earth? Let them intervene and help us solve the problems of the earth! The essential task on Earth is to put an end to misery, hunger, unemployment, and war; to give to everyone access to a dignified life and lay the bases for human fraternity."

This is the avowed purpose of the Fourth International Posadist, based in Brussels: to suppress the capitalist system, and to destroy nuclear weapons and all the military power they convey, all to establish socialism on Earth. But this grand goal can be achieved only by forging alliances with classless societies in cyberspace. As the theorist Juan Posadas puts it: "When beings from other planets come along, we must call on them to intervene and collaborate with us for the suppression of misery."

Ultimately, posadists seem to have rein-vented Christianity: to combat injustice on Earth, there is nothing quite like an intervention from above. The most fanatic of supporters, on the verge of causing schism or split, note several messiahs in the history of the social revolution: Marx, Engels, Lenin, and Trotsky were allegedly extraterrestrial interlopers, practicing the art of infiltration and revolutionary elitism to help their comrades on Earth.

49° 10' 5" N, 6° 52' 8" E

THE MORSBACH FLYING SAUCER

MOSELLE (FRANCE)

On October 7, 1954, at 8:30 p.m., a delivery truck suddenly stopped in front of the Forbach Police Station, in the Lorraine region of France. The driver, Charles Bou, made a statement: "Tonight, at 7:20 p.m., I was coming from Rosbruck in my Citroën van, heading for Morsbach.

"On arrival at the New bridge, located about 131 feet (40 meters) from the crossroads of the RN 3 highway and the road to Cocheren, I saw an illuminated line on the road.

"Believing it to be an accident, and the police to be present, I slowed down and continued carefully until I was about 33 feet (10 meters) away from the light in question. I had my headlights dimmed.

"At one point, I noticed a vehicle that obstructed the road almost entirely. The craft was the shape of a large oval of about 26 feet (8 meters) and 13 feet (4 meters) tall. Along its perimeter there were about ten beams of light, pointing toward the ground. These beams originated in the center of the craft and were spaced about 11 to 16 inches (30 to 40 centimeters) apart. The range of these beams was between 31 to 39 inches (80 to 100 centimeters).

"Astonished to encounter such an obstacle on the road, I stopped my van (put into neutral) and opened the driver's door.

"With some apprehension, I set my foot on the ground just when the craft, which I believe to be a flying saucer, rose vertically to about 50 feet (15 meters) above, and then flew off toward the southwest, somewhere between Morsbach and Cocheren."

Despite the lack of further eyewitness accounts, the police officers took this testimony seriously. They questioned his boss, who confirmed that Charles Bou "is well regarded and generally not a braggart." This trustworthy witness, moreover, repeated his story to higher-rank officers without contradicting himself. He even displayed a rare amount of precision: "The craft itself was a petrol blue color. When it set off, the beams lit up, initially in a milky color, and then turned lilac-blue.

> The craft was the shape of a large oval. Along its perimeter, there were about ten beams of light.

"The craft moved noiselessly. I neither felt a draft nor did I perceive smoke. . . . The craft took no more than four seconds to disappear with incredible speed."

The police officers drew up a sketch of the encounter, as well as a diagram of the spacecraft, and sent these, along with their report, to the vice president of the French Council of Ministers and minister of defense, Emmanuel Temple. Did he, a former aviator, care about the dossier? What we know is that he would, in the months to follow, urge the government of Pierre Mendès France to acquire nuclear weapons. As for Charles Bou's observations, they are among the archival treasures preserved today by the Historical Service of the French Ministry of Defense, hidden behind the thick walls of the Château de Vincennes.

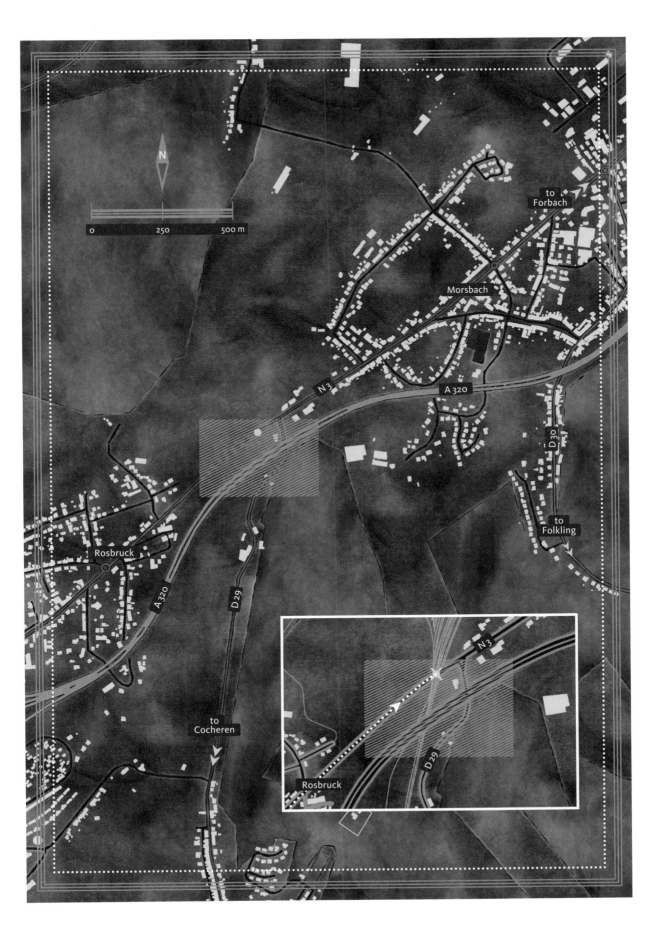

N

0   250   500 m

to
Forbach

Morsbach

N 3

A 320

D 30

to
Folkling

Rosbruck

A 320

D 29

to
Cocheren

N 3

D 29

Rosbruck

47° 12' 45" N, 5° 11' 2" E

THE STAR OF MARLIENS

CÔTE-D'OR (FRANCE)

The man who, on May 10, 1967, alerted the Genlis police officers was not a simple farmer: Émile Maillotte was the mayor of Marliens, a farming village of about eighty inhabitants in the French Côte-d'Or. The mayor did not see a UFO, but he was alerted by a rather strange "upheaval of the soil" in a clover field on his farm: the Terraillot field, on the edge of country road D25.

Covering an area of about 50 square feet (15 square meters), there was "a figure made up of a convex polygon, with six furrows radiating from its center where the surface of the soil split." This six-pointed star appeared to be embossed onto the earth, but without the geometric regularity commonly found in crop circles. It was a rather softly drawn, sprawling star within which the soil appeared to have been scorched: "The central section of these stirred earthworks seems to have withstood very high pressure; it is hard and very compacted as if it were dehydrated," reads the police report, which further notes seven cylindrical imprints of 8 by 16 inches (20 by 40 centimeters), as if a spacecraft had docked in the clover field or had sunk probes into the ground.

Even more strange, the presence of "grainy matter whose shade ranges from gray to purple" was observed inside the star—a matter completely foreign to the local geology. A Geiger counter "passed through the churned-up soil" found no trace of radioactivity, but the chemical analysis of samples taken surprised the experts: "The soil samples submitted for examination are partially covered by an extremely faint purplish-white deposit, which, when examined under a microscope, has the appearance of fine particles that appear to have undergone partial fusion. This is in formal contradiction with the absence of any trace of fire on the imprint left in the field, as evidenced by its vegetation, which simply dried but did not carbonize."

> The central section of these stirred earthworks seems to have withstood very high pressure.

The very thorough investigation of these mysterious observations eventually led to the technical inspector of air traffic in Dijon being called the next day by his counterpart at Orly airport, Mr. Bois, who asked for his advice as to what happened in Marliens: "Mr. Bois told me that an unidentified echo had been tracked on the military radar in Creil and that this suggests that an unidentified object had hovered over Pontoise for about an hour."

The coat of arms of Marliens now features a shining sun surrounded by three clovers.

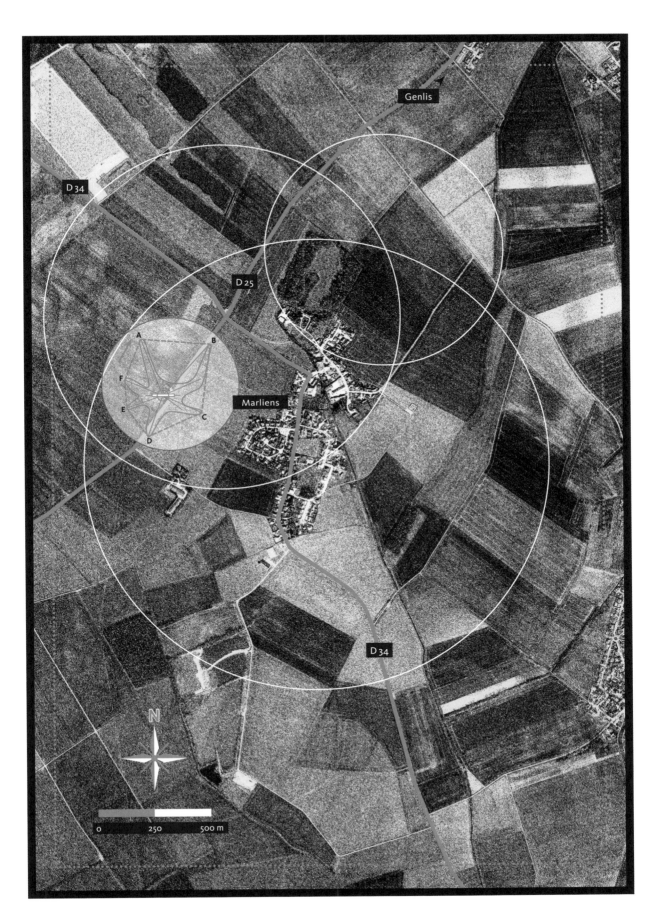

Genlis

D 34

D 25

A   B

F

E   C

D

Marliens

D 34

N

0   250   500 m

44° 53' 57" N, 5° 1' 13" E

THE CHABEUIL DOUBLE

DRÔME (FRANCE)

On September 26, 1954, despite the murky weather, Lucette Leboeuf and her husband went to the Chabeuil cemetery to lay flowers at the family vault. While he stayed there to clean up the grave, she went for a walk around the area.

Outside Valence in southeastern France, on the edge of the Vercors Massif, Chabeuil is one of these small towns that has preserved its rural charm. Lucette was picking mulberries, accompanied by her cocker spaniel Dolly, a black dog happy to frolic in the neighboring fields. "As Dolly, the dog, returned to me, she suddenly stopped and started to bay at the moon," Lucette testified. "The dogs in the neighboring houses, who were all tied up, were also howling at the moon. When I then raised my head, I saw a small being about 8 feet (2.5 meters) away from me, coming out of the cornfield." The field had only about a dozen rows, and what emerged from these defies all imagination: "A small being of 3 feet, 6 inches to 3 feet, 8 inches (1 meter, 10 centimeters to 1 meter, 15 centimeters) that seemed wrapped in a transparent spacesuit from head to toe." Did they look into each other's eyes? At first, Lucette said they did, before explaining that the helmet was "blurred," so you could not see the face. However, she was definite about the absence of gestures: "Its arms were not visible," she said, "which is not to say that it did not have any." Retractable arms, then, because the spacesuit, since it was transparent, would have allowed one to see the limbs of this being that she compared to a "scarecrow." Something is confusing about it, however, and her account is obviously overshadowed by her fear.

"I screamed and hid in the hedge, the fear making my teeth chatter, as it moved toward me, jumping." Then, "from the field behind the square cornfield rose a saucer-like spacecraft resembling a large mechanical spinning top for children but with a flat bottom," the poor witness went on to tell, having been unable to discern any lights or portholes. "It rose slowly and hovered above the cornfield—I noticed a slight humming during this—then it tilted by 90 degrees and disappeared in a northeast direction at a dizzying speed while emitting a strange whistling sound."

> A small being of 3 feet, 6 inches to 3 feet, 8 inches (1 meter, 10 centimeters to 1 meter, 15 centimeters) that seemed wrapped in a transparent spacesuit from head to toe.

The neighbors heard the noise as well, as did Mr. Leboeuf, busy in the cemetery, as did three farmers who were surprised to find Lucette lying immobile in the bushes. "We are unable to determine whether the witness's paralysis was due to fear or an effect caused

Montélier

N

Valence

Malissard

Cemetery

Chabeuil

Montvendre

o   500 m

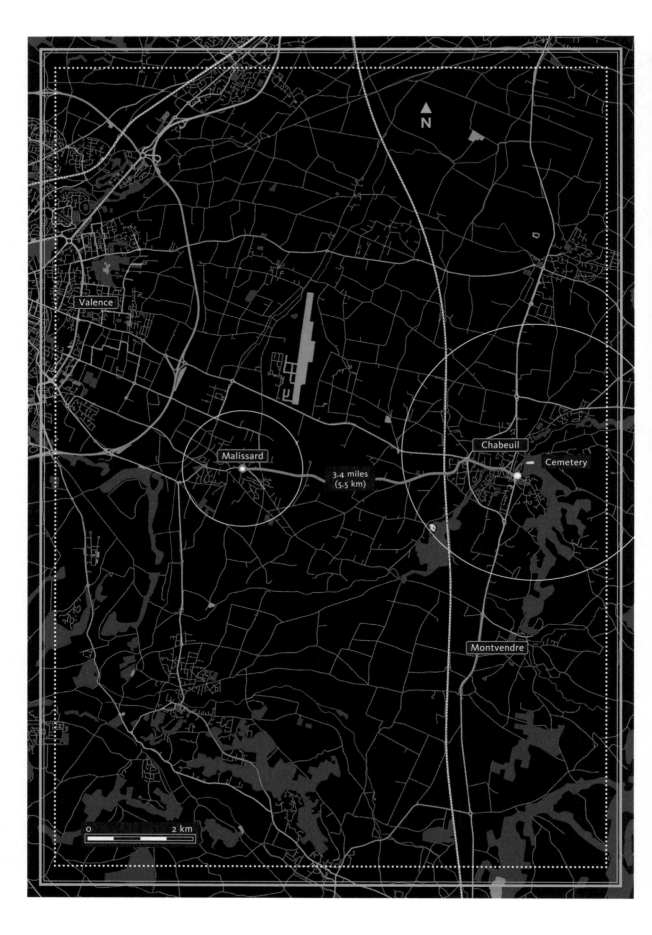

N

Valence

Malissard

3.4 miles
(5.5 km)

Chabeuil

Cemetery

Montvendre

0   2 km

by the craft," the investigators of the Ufological Association of the Drôme would note, who conveyed their findings to GEPAN, which stands for "Groupe d'études des phénomènes aérospatiaux non" (the Unidentified Aerospace Phenomenon Research Group), a division within the French space agency CNES, headquartered in Toulouse. GEPAN was also told that the poor woman remained in bed with a fever and in a state of alarming physical disorder for two days. As for Dolly, she trembled for three days and three nights straight.

> In fact, 1.5 miles (2.5 kilometers) from the cornfield where the "scarecrow" appeared, a new landing had been reported!

This testimony might have easily gone unnoticed among the many observations made in France during the "wave of 1954." Sixteen days earlier, for example, a certain Marius Dewilde saw two beings similar to that of Chabeuil, without apparent arms, in front of his house in Quarouble, near the Belgian border. The day after the encounter, four children in the village of Prémanon in the Jura département found themselves in the presence of a

strange shining "ghost," who disappeared when ordered to by a luminous red ball. The police officers would find four regular holes in the ground and a 13-foot-diameter (4 meter) circle within which the grass was flattened. And if you added to these encounters with animate beings the mere signals of UFOs in the sky, the map would cover all of France.

But a quarter of a century later, the police station's intelligence office and GEPAN corresponded with regard to unearthing Lucette Leboeuf's witness account. In fact, 1.5 miles (2.5 kilometers) from the cornfield where the "scarecrow" appeared, a new landing had been reported! On March 3, 1978, at approximately 7:30 p.m., a motorist and her two children, traveling between Mélisard and Chabeuil, saw a shining yellow-orange vessel in a field: "A kind of banana, with the tips facing down," but with two portholes "in the shape of windows with rounded corners." The young woman courageously stopped her Citroën 2CV to walk down the trail; the spacecraft, without producing any noise, took off and disappeared southward.

Such a double occurrence, twenty-four years apart, is absolutely exceptional in the annals of ufology. Since then, Chabeuil has been awaiting its third visit of the little being without arms that Lucette described as "a kid in cellophane."

44° 45' 41" N, 1° 8' 32" W

THE UFO PORT OF ARÈS

GIRONDE (FRANCE)

UFOs are not welcome everywhere. In Châteauneuf-du-Pape, a municipal decree stipulates that "the flight, landing, and takeoff of aircraft known as "flying saucers" or "flying cigars" of any nationality are prohibited on the territory of this municipality." According to article 2, "any aircraft designated as 'flying saucer' or 'flying cigar' that lands on the territory of the municipality will be immediately towed"—a task article 3 entrusts to the local guard. . . . This text was signed by the town's dry-witted mayor, Lucien Jeume, on October 25, 1954: amid a wave of observations, the ban caused somewhat of a splash at the time. Despite its somewhat discriminatory character, the decree is still in force today.

> The initiative was approved by the town council to welcome travelers through the universe to our planet.

The town of Arès, in the Gironde region in southwestern France, on the Arcachon Bay, is more welcoming in this regard. There, the bias has worked in the aliens' favor since a certain Robert Cotten, known as "Bob," an electronics technician at Mérignac airport and passionate about space issues, launched a petition in 1976. "If we never see UFOs, it is because we don't have a place to welcome them," he logically concluded. The mayor at the time, Christian Raymond,

agreed with him—especially after Cotton stressed the appeal of a landing spot for space visitors to tourists in the middle of a UFO-spotting craze. Moreover, the town was also known for the mystical "revelations" by visionary Michel Potay, whose house had become a place of pilgrimage and worship for his fanatic disciples: a site dedicated to aliens would backfire on them while offering lovers of paranormal activity a more family-friendly attraction.

This is how the UFO port of Arès was inaugurated on August 15, 1976. Not only are they exempt from any kind of landing fee, but the extraterrestrials in the vessels are even invited to local events: petanque tournaments, gathering seafood by hand, oyster festivals. . . . Besides a plain landing strip, the UFO port has been equipped with a windsock and beacons, and, in 2010, a sculpture in the shape of a spaceship. The latter, eroded by the sea winds, was replaced in June 2016 by a brand-new flying saucer, inspired by the French movie *The Cabbage Soup*. The initiative has become a source of envy, so much so that the municipalities of Bocaiuva do Sul in Brazil and Lajas in Puerto Rico have expressed their intention to build similar UFO ports.

In Arès, a marble stele recalls that the initiative was "approved by the town council to welcome travelers through the universe to our planet"—but it also features a slight regret, written in the Gascon dialect: Que vos atendem totjorn—We are still waiting for you . . .

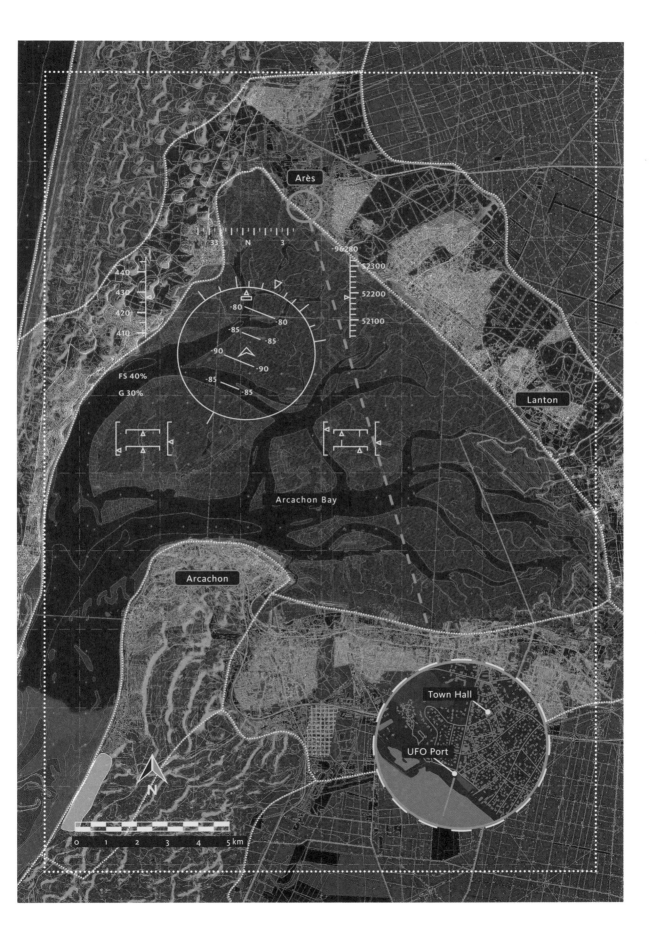

Arès

33 N 3

-96280

52300

52200

52100

440

430

420

410

-80

-80

-85

-85

-90

-90

-85

-85

FS 40%

G 30%

Lanton

Arcachon Bay

Arcachon

Town Hall

UFO Port

N

0   1   2   3   4   5 km

55° 45' 35" N, 37° 37' 33" E

THE UMMITE HQ

MOSCOW (RUSSIA)

The story began in Madrid, at a bar called the Happy Whale, the regular meeting place of the Friends of Space Visitors, an association of enthusiastic ufologists. From 1966 onward, one of them, Fernando Sesma, started to receive fascinating letters that he read to the group.

These mailings seemed like they were written by earthlings, but they really originated from the planet Ummo and were sent through its infiltrators on Earth. At least that is what the Ummites themselves wrote in their abundant correspondence: having discovered Earth by chance, by capturing the mayday call of a Norwegian liner, they sent out a scientific mission to study our planet. Passing through the 14.4 light-years that separate us from their advanced civilization, these benevolent visitors apparently landed on March 28, 1950, in the vicinity of Digne, France, before blending in with humankind, whom they judged harshly.

Humanity seemed to them to be backward, fragmented, and poorly organized. The Ummites, however, would intervene only in cases of grave danger, such as that posed by nuclear war, but they did allow themselves to caution earthlings against themselves by addressing the most conscious of them directly—those in receipt of these letters. Sesma and his friends, as well as other ufologists in various countries, received thousands of pages in total. The "Ummite revelation" gave them a glimpse of a more advanced, happier society that had reached a high level of technology thanks to collectivist organization.

In his 1993 book *L'Affaire Ummo, les extra-terrestres qui venaid du froid* ("The Ummo case: The aliens coming from the cold"), Renaud Marhic developed a very political thesis: the Ummites were the result of manipulation by the Soviet secret service, eager to spread pacifist and socialist ideals throughout the Western world. Ummo, in short, did not exist outside the Lubyanka Building, the imposing and sinister Moscow headquarters of the former KGB, and the seat of the current FSB.

> The Ummites would intervene only in cases of grave danger, such as that posed by nuclear war, but they did allow themselves to caution earthlings against themselves.

In 1992, however, the Spaniard José Luis Jordán Peña admitted before the Guardia Civil to be the author of the hoax: the term "Ummo" was derived from humo, "smoke" in Spanish. The author of these initial letters continued to deceive ufologists for twenty-five years, until the joke got out of control. Other forgers, even sects, had also started to boast about the mailings, giving rise to the huge corpora on the Ummo-Science website. The Frenchman Dominique Caudron, for his part, lambasted in a book what he calls the "Ummoristes" . . .

Ignoring this malicious gossip, the Ummites continue to write to us: they are now communicating in tweets . . .

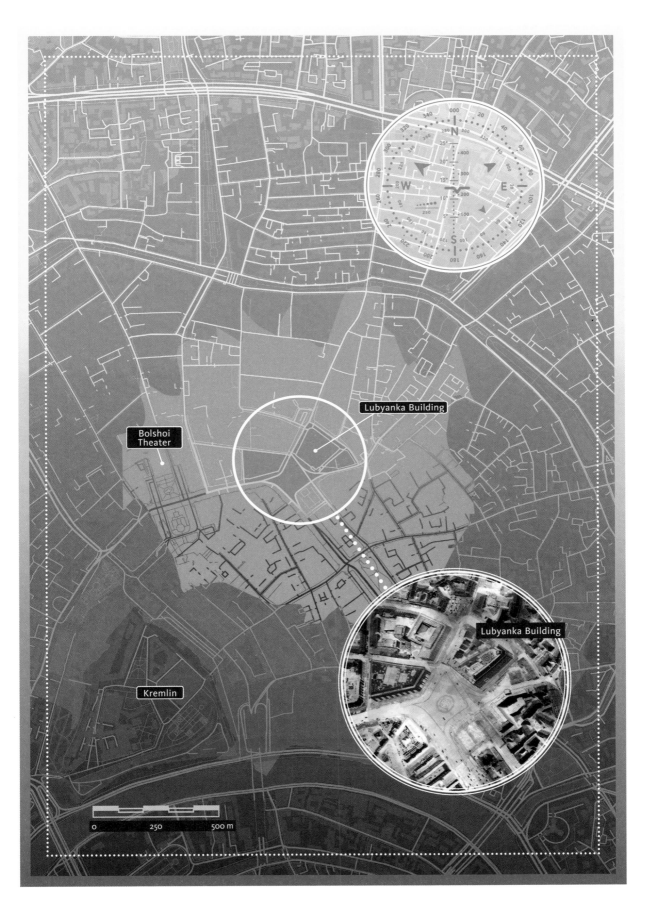

Bolshoi
Theater

Lubyanka Building

Lubyanka Building

Kremlin

0   250   500 m

Bandiagara Esarpment

AFRICA

Antananarivo

14° 30' 0" N, 3° 30' 0" W

THE CHILDREN OF SIRIUS

BANDIAGARA ESCARPMENT (MALI)

The theory of the ancient astronauts, when applied to the African continent, has focused mainly on ancient Egypt and its pyramids, arguing that their construction indicates the use of technical means from cyberspace. But there is another people, who still exist today, whose traditions intrigue ufologists as well: the Dogon people.

This tribe lives in an area stretching from the extremely barren landscape of the Bandiagara Escarpment to the bend of the Niger River in Mali. There are only seven hundred thousand members left today, who have kept their culture alive while keeping up a facade of adopted Islam or Christianity. Their cosmogony and mythology have surprised ethnologists: according to Marcel Griaule in 1950 and Robert K. G. Temple, later on, they claim to originate from another planet, Po Tolo, an orbiting star in the Sirius system.

Sirius can easily be spotted with the naked eye in winter, since the star shines brightly at night. But the Dogons have long known what Western science discovered only in 1862; namely, that Sirius is not a single star like the sun: it is made up of at least two light foci, Sirius A and Sirius B, not to mention the hypothetical Sirius C. The Dogon do not have access to any elaborate equipment for observing stars and planets, but they have long known about the sphericity of the earth, the rings of Saturn, and the main moons of Jupiter. Moreover, initiated members of the Awa society express themselves in a secret language, "Sigi so," to convey this secret knowledge.

Transcripts by Griaule and Temple—which have been challenged by other researchers—argue that Po Tolo orbited around a "companion" star of Sirius from which the Dogons' ancestors had left, following their master Nommo. What is more disturbing still is that Dogon priests say their ancestors were amphibians: Nommo's flying arch landed on the water, and its occupants lived first as fish people before their environment gradually dried up to become the desert it is today.

> Their cosmogony and mythology have surprised ethnologists: they claim to originate from another planet, from Po Tolo, an orbiting star in the Sirius system.

For their ritual celebrations, the children of Sirius display superb masks made from shells that look like space helmets with towering antennae. Their traditional dried-clay houses are decorated with geometric patterns and glowing cowrie shells as well as lightbulbs and buttons, inevitably evoking science-fiction architecture. They used whatever means they had on hand to re-create bold lines and bright lights. Like all shipwrecked people, perhaps the Sirians of the country of the Dogon were seeking to communicate with their distant cousins in outer space?

18° 42' 18" N, 46° 49' 31" E

THE FLYING CIGAR OF TANANARIVE

ANTANANARIVO (MADAGASCAR)

UFOs come in waves: after the wave of 1947, the sightings became fewer until the extraordinary "Great Wave of 1954" that flooded the world. Flashing lights and strange phenomena were spotted in the United States, Brazil, and Thailand, while thousands of reports were recorded in France alone.

However, in 1954, "France" would, for a few more years, refer to a vast empire. Its colonies would soon become independent, but the "flying saucers" fever still spread across the territory, and on August 16, 1954, at around 6 p.m., a colossal spacecraft flew over Tananarive—present-day Antananarivo—the capital of Madagascar, the "Great Island" in the Indian Ocean in the Southern Hemisphere.

First, there was a big ball of "electric green" light that illuminated the cloudless sky, but observers soon noticed that this entirely immaterial "incandescent lenticular mass" only preceded a huge metal-looking spindle, which in turn was followed by flying red sparks. At the same time, a general power outage brought the city to a halt. These observations were later transmitted to metropolitan France by a select witness: Edmond Campagnac, a professional pilot and graduate of the prestigious École Polytechnique, then serving as the technical manager of Air France in Tananarive.

The craft he described was not a saucer as such, but a "flying cigar," one of those oblong, rounded aircraft that look like ancient blimps—and were typical of the 1954 wave. Their size fueled the earthlings' fears: people wondered if the aliens had not simply come on a recce aboard smaller spaceships in 1947, before sending their jumbo aircrafts full of invaders and technically advanced equipment later on.

> On August 16, 1954, at around 6 p.m., a colossal spacecraft flew over Tananarive, the capital of Madagascar.

A long while later, in 1969, Edmond Campagnac was invited to the French TV program *Dossiers de l'écran*, a very popular debating show. After the broadcast, avid readers of the ufologist journal *Lumières dans la nuit* managed to get hold of the switchboard index cards listing viewers' calls to the show. To their surprise, they found listed former colonial subjects or Malagasy people, several of whom had witnessed the phenomenon of Tananarive. Thanks to an unparalleled survey that went on until 1990, these witnesses were tracked down and their stories recorded. Such a long time after the event, these witnesses did not all describe the same route in the sky, but their testimonies agree on the appearance of the spacecraft: the green beam that preceded it, and the glowing cloud that escorted it . . .

"The craft was a dark mass that stood out from the clear sky," said the retired chief

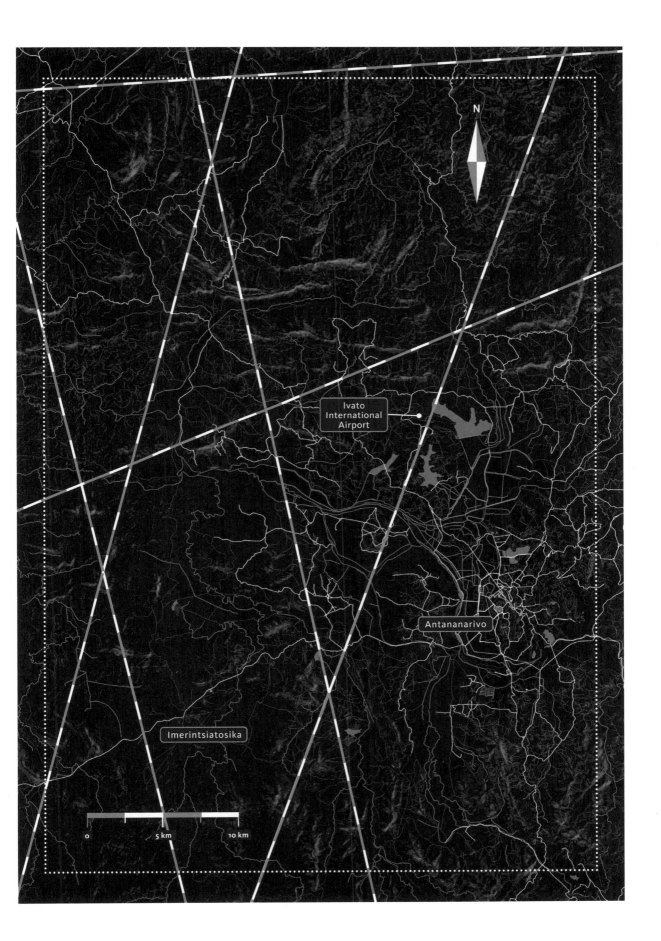

N

Ivato
International
Airport

Antananarivo

Imerintsiatosika

0   5 km   10 km

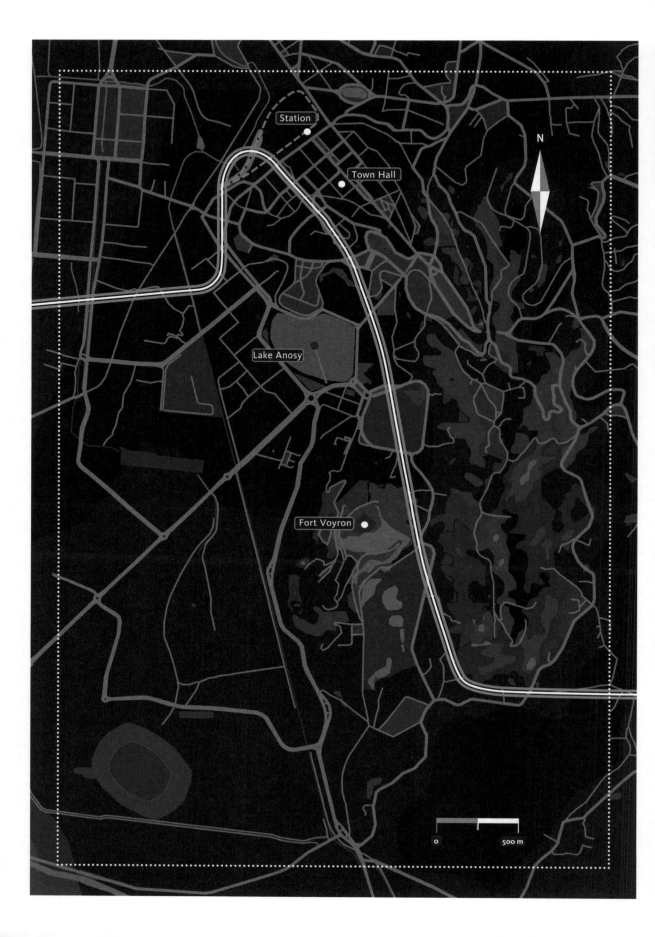

Station

Town Hall

Lake Anosy

Fort Voyron

N

0   500 m

warrant officer and former artilleryman Grimout, who estimated the spaceship to have been about 328 feet (100 meters) in length: "There were a dozen lights, like lit-up portholes. At the rear of the craft, there was a trail of blue, dark-red, and white stars, like the sparks emitted when grinding a piece of iron. Length of these sparks: double the craft, so 492 to 656 feet (150 to 200 meters)."

> It was a very luminous object, in the shape of a cigar of about 98 to 131 feet (30 to 40 meters), trailed by some red sparks.

Jeanne Rafaramalala Noro, then secretary at the Tana town hall, remembers the arrival and its date very well, since it was her birthday: "My attention was drawn to a very bright flying object, green in color, a few meters from the city hall gates and just above my head, about 328 feet (100 meters) away. The sky was very clear, without a single cloud. The streets were thronged with people because it was the end of the working day. This object was flying very quickly and without making a noise. I was very afraid since I had never seen such an object. . . . It was a very luminous object, in the shape of a cigar of about 98 to 131 feet (30 to 40 meters), trailed by some red sparks. I don't recall if this object had portholes, but I was very afraid and was hiding under a tree. This object caused a panicked roar around Tananarive." According to the photographer Georges Rafalimanana, who unfortunately did not have his camera with him at the time, it was "an oval-shaped object, bright orange in color, trailed by several red and blindingly bright sparks" that moved "very quickly and without making a noise."

These observations are especially valuable since, in Madagascar, explanations for the sightings that draw on a Cold War context do not hold. The French did not conduct any air tests here, the Soviets were a long way off, and the US base at Diego Garcia, in the neighboring Chagos archipelago, was opened only in 1966. There have so far been no rational interpretations that could explain the phenomenon of the "flying cigar" of Tananarive, that spectacular UFO that went on a mission to the land of the lemurs.

Baïkonour

Byurakan

Canaan

ASIA

Tunguska

Agartha

31° 2' 45" N, 34° 51' 5" E

LOST TRIBES FROM OUTER SPACE

CANAAN (ISRAEL)

The theory of the ancient astronauts could not leave out the Hebrews, an ancient people whose writings are full of aerospace phenomena. Doesn't the Bible, in particular, make mention of two cities, Sodom and Gomorrah, razed to the ground by the fires sent from heaven? And what about the "burning bush" Moses encountered? Not to mention the prophet Elijah rising to the heavens on "a chariot and horses of fire" . . .

Moreover, ufologists emphasize a peculiarity of the Scripture, where the entity usually translated with the single word "God" is more often referred to by the plural Hebrew terms of Elohim or Adonai. If the Jews were truly monotheistic, they should have written the singular Eloha or Adon, for the "Lord." Is it a royal "we" or poetic license to glorify the Creator? Not at all! We should really interpret the verses in the Holy Bible literally when they tell us about the exploits of the "masters," the "lords"—that is, of aliens who came to civilize the earth in time immemorial. As for Jehovah or Yahweh, which derives from the letters YHWH, would it not be naive and misleading to humanize this acronym designating a mysterious force?

Thus, in this highly heretical reinterpretation of Genesis, it is no longer the "Spirit of God" that was hovering over the face of the waters, but the "wind of the Elohim"; that is, the turboprops of their ancient saucers. And it is no longer right to say that the "sons of God" took wives, but rather the descendants of those space warriors were mixing their genes with those of the earthlings. From this union sprang the "chosen people," the only one capable of preserving its unity and age-old traditions throughout time . . .

> Jews are not from this earth and that is why they have always been oppressed.

That is what Marc Dem's 1976 essay *Lost Tribes from Outer Space* (translated by Lowell Bair, 1977) claims, tracing the singularity of the children of Israel to their extraterrestrial origin. The seminarist turned journalist, who goes by the real name of Marc Demeulenaere, defended himself against accusations of anti-Semitism, even though his book is worth detailed analysis in this respect: "Jews are not from this earth and that is why they have always been oppressed by other people, as it happens with organ transplants when we witness the phenomenon of rejection," he states. Later in life, returning to Catholicism in its most traditional expression, he regretted that his "fable" had been taken at face value, and tried to wipe out the remaining copies of his book, which have become rare today.

The notion of the extraterrestrial origin of the Elohim recurs in the belief of the Raëlists, and it is indeed in Jerusalem that their guru, Claude Vorilhon—known as Raël, "the Messenger"—planned to establish his extraterrestrial embassy.

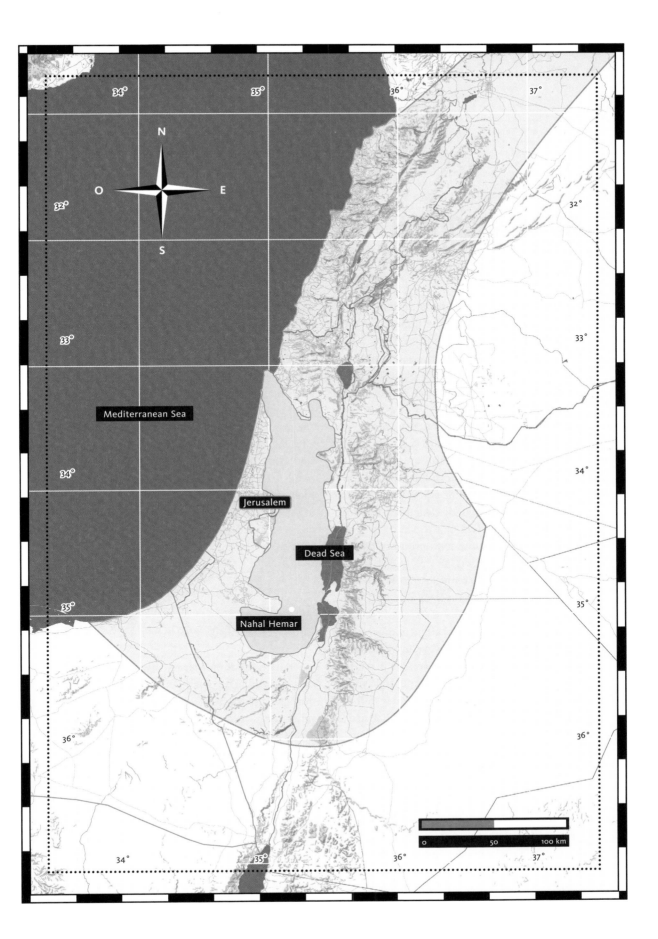

N

O   E

S

Mediterranean Sea

Jerusalem

Dead Sea

Nahal Hemar

0   50   100 km

60° 55' 1" N, 101° 56' 56" E

OGDY'S WRATH

TUNGUSKA (SIBERIA)

On a beautiful summer's morning, life was buzzing in all parts of the Siberian forest, and the hunters of the Evenks people respectfully invoked Ogdy, the god of light and fire: they were preparing for a plentiful hunt in these parts full of game on the stony banks of the Tunguska River, a tributary of the Yenisey River, far from any Russian town or farm, 37 miles (60 kilometers) from the village of Vanavara. That is when the apocalypse struck.

It is June 30, 1908—or rather, June 17, according to the Julian calendar, still in use at the time in tsarist Russia. From the clear sky, a huge fireball dropped, which in the space of a few moments produced an extraordinary blast. At the point of impact, all life was wiped out, and within a radius of 12.4 miles (20 kilometers), millions of trees were knocked over, broken like matches. Within a radius of 62 miles (100 kilometers), the event still left behind unprecedented devastation, and the shock wave, unlike anything ever in human history, was even felt in western Europe and North America. The atmosphere hung full of ash and cinder, so much so that it would knock the world's climate off balance for months to come.

It would take years for the first scientific expedition to reach the epicenter of the cataclysm, in 1927. Neither a volcano nor methane deposits can explain the phenomenon, since it did not come from underground. There is no crater either, unless you assume that Lake Cheko is the result of the impact. But abundant cosmic dust and metal beads are scattered over the ravaged forest. What hit this place, causing such damage without distorting the soil?

Could a celestial body have disintegrated, a giant meteorite dislodged, a comet of frozen gases melted in record time, dispersing its sublimate material into a rain of natural projectiles? Did a small asteroid burst there, something like a tiny black hole? By default, scientists speak of the "TCB," the Tunguska cosmic body, to give a name to the unidentified meteor that was eventually nicknamed Ogdy, in reference to the god of the Evenks. In memory of this event, the UN declared June 30 International Asteroid Day.

> From the clear sky, a huge fireball dropped, which in the space of a few moments produced an extraordinary blast.

For Russian ufologists, there is no doubt that astronomers would have seen or even predicted the course of such a star, even if it was small. Ogdy, however, surprised everyone, so it must have been of a different nature. Was it a shipwrecked vessel? A nuclear test conducted by an extraterrestrial civilization? The warning of a distant power? There is no lack of theories, providing fodder for science fiction novels and video games. A century later, a new forest has sprouted on the banks of the Tunguska River, but Ogdy's wrath may have been calmed only for a while . . .

Strelka-Chunya

N
W   E
S

Lake Cheko

15.5 miles (25 km)

50 km

Tunguska

Vanavara

TCB's trajectory

0   10   20   30 km

46° 51' 44" N, 103° 50' 47" E

THE INTRATERRESTRIAL PORTAL

AGARTHA (MONGOLIA)

Extraterrestrials are only one hypothesis, counterbalanced by an even more preposterous assumption: the existence of "intraterrestrials"; that is, of intelligent and organized biological entities living inside our planet—as Hollow Earth theories would have it. These hypotheses diverge when it comes to the origins of these cave-dwelling nations, with some assuming human roots, and others seeing them as clearly distinct from humans. Nothing is stopping the latter believers from imagining that intraterrestrials have descended from ancient extraterrestrials, lurking underground and awaiting reinforcements to take control of the entire earth.

> Science has there developed calmly and nothing is threatened with destruction. The subterranean people have reached the highest knowledge.

To find out, one would have to come into contact with our surprisingly discreet underground neighbors, which would require gateways between our habitat and theirs. Penetrating the concentric circles of the earth's landmass was the great aim of US Army captain John Cleves Symmes in the early nineteenth century. But the so-called Symmes holes, which were supposedly masked by polar ice, were never found.

By accident, the Russian Revolution reopened Pandora's box when it put Ferdynand Ossendowski on the roads in 1920. A former finance minister in the counterrevolutionary Kerensky government, he sought to escape the Bolsheviks by crossing Siberia and Mongolia. That is where he heard of the hidden land of Agartha, the enigmatic underground monarchy that apparently housed the "King of the World."

"More than sixty thousand years ago a Holyman disappeared with a whole tribe of people under the ground and never appeared again on the surface of the earth," he reported in *Beasts, Men and Gods* (translated by Lewis Stanton Palen), quoting a legend relayed by Buddhist lamas. "No one knows where this place is. One says Afghanistan, others India. All the people there are protected against Evil and crimes do not exist within its bournes. Science has there developed calmly and nothing is threatened with destruction. The subterranean people have reached the highest knowledge."

According to Ossendowski, these dark-skinned tribes were thrust from Agartha "and returned to the earth, bringing with them the mystery of predictions according to cards, grasses and the lines of the palm." If these "Gypsies" were able to get out of the center of the earth, it must be possible to enter, but no one seems to have regained access to the inner world and its highly developed civilization.

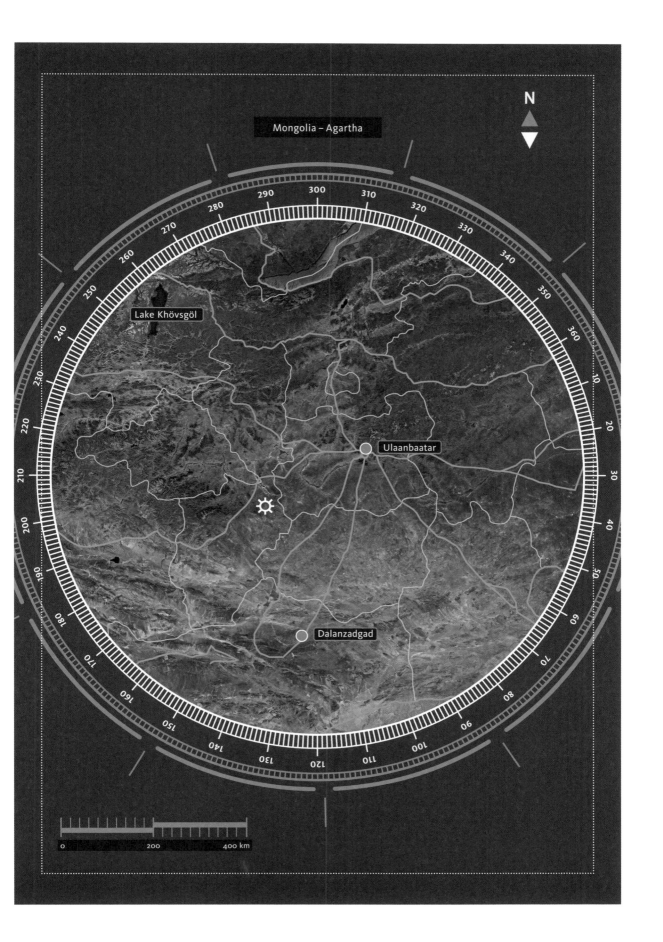

N

Mongolia – Agartha

Lake Khövsgöl

Ulaanbaatar

Dalanzadgad

0   200   400 km

40° 20' 14" N, 44° 16' 19" E

THE SUPERCIVILIZATIONS OBSERVATORY

BYURAKAN (ARMENIA)

High up in the Caucasus, the Byurakan Observatory scans the skies, driven by a particular fear. This is where, in 1964, the most ambitious conference for Soviet space exploration was held, to update on traces of extraterrestrial life and conditions of trade with potential exocivilizations.

> Type II civilizations can consume the energy of a star, and Type III civilizations can harness the energy of their entire galaxy

The SETI project (short for Search for Extraterrestrial Intelligence) began in the West, where, in 1961, Western researchers gained the pole position at the Green Bank conference, held at the eponymous observatory in West Virginia, USA. Three years later, Byurakan organized a repeat for the Eastern Bloc, but what might have been a mere propaganda stunt suddenly took on a new dimension, due to the intervention of a young professor, Nikolai Semyonovich Kardashev.

Born on April 25, 1932, in Moscow, the astrophysicist did not claim to have seen flying saucers or even to have picked up a signal. Trained in the Soviet schooling system, he only wanted to understand scientific methods, and that is how he articulated a type of abstract reasoning with which everybody agreed.

If "supercivilizations" exist—and no one can rule this out a priori—they can be classified into three categories, he argued, according to the energy they are able to use. A Type I civilization can harness the energy produced by its planet: this is the stage the world's population is about to reach in the industrial age. Type II civilizations can consume the energy of a star, and Type III civilizations can harness the energy of their entire galaxy.

The "Kardachev scale," in its simplicity, poses the problem of exocivilizations in new terms; it highlights the technological gap that would separate us from more technologically advanced visitors, while indicating what developmental level a society must achieve to consider space expansion. Often commented on, supplemented, and refuted, the Kardashev scale remains at the center of current reflections on interstellar communication.

Since Armenia regained independence, the Byurakan Observatory no longer has the same amount of funds available as in the days of the USSR. Its astrophysicists are trying to overcome administrative problems while waiting to capture the signal of a Type III supercivilization.

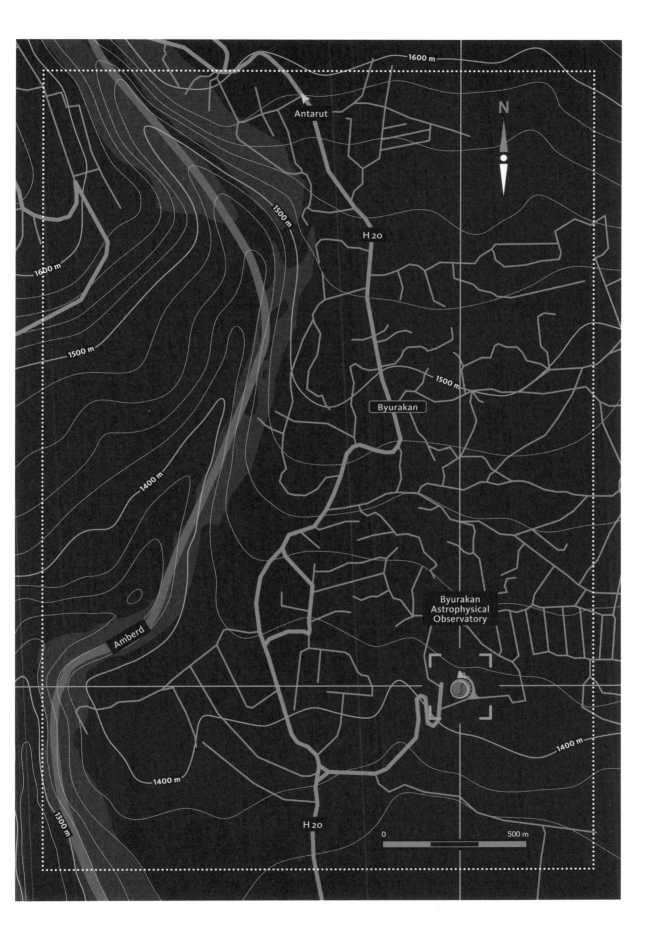

Antarut

H2O

N

1600 m

1500 m

1600 m

1500 m

1500 m

Byurakan

1400 m

Amberd

Byurakan
Astrophysical
Observatory

1400 m

1400 m

1300 m

H2O

0   500 m

60° 55' 1" N, 101° 56' 56" E

THE SPIED-ON COSMODROME

BAIKONUR (KAZAKHSTAN)

Since the breakup of the USSR, the city of Baikonur belongs to the Republic of Kazakhstan, but the Russians remain its principal users: the launch facility and the city are administered by Russia, while having to comply with Kazak laws, and the mayor is jointly appointed by both countries.

Baikonur was formerly known as Leninsk, and the army began construction of the cosmodrome in 1955, in a deserted part of the Kazak steppe. Only one special railway route connects it with the rest of the world. The original aim was to launch intercontinental missiles from the spaceport, but over the years the Red Army's secret base has developed into a space launch center: this is where Sputnik 1 was launched in 1957, and later the rocket that in 1961 projected the first human into orbit, Yuri Gagarin. In memory of the latter, space flight candidates urinate at the left rear wheel of the coach before takeoff, following the example of their Soviet hero back in the day.

Despite their isolation, such strategic facilities do not fail to attract the interest of rival powers, which is why the US, in the middle of the Cold War, managed to obtain aerial photographs taken by its U-2 spy plane that took off from Pakistan.

Those times seemed to be over when, on July 1, 1993, the launch of the Soyuz TM-17 rocket was disrupted by the appearance of a "bright orange spot quite clearly visible to the naked eye" in the sky, according to the witness account of Frenchman Robert Macé, who was present on the day. "All I can say is that the local technicians looked frankly worried at the time, and then everything went back to normal and relaxed again after 20 minutes," said another Frenchman, Paul Ramage, also on-site. Among the Russians, their tour guide, Valentin Zotov, looked nervous before making a joke: "The same Zotov, in the coach taking us from the cosmodrome to the hotel in Leninsk, was kidding and told us that 'the little green men came to watch the launch.'"

> The launch of the Soyuz TM-17 rocket was disrupted by the appearance of a "bright orange spot quite clearly visible to the naked eye" in the sky.

Officially, a panel had come loose from the launcher and created the illusion of a stealth bomber in the sky, but this trivial explanation does not satisfy ufologists: if earthlings take off from Baikonur to conquer space, why would aliens not be interested in such a base?

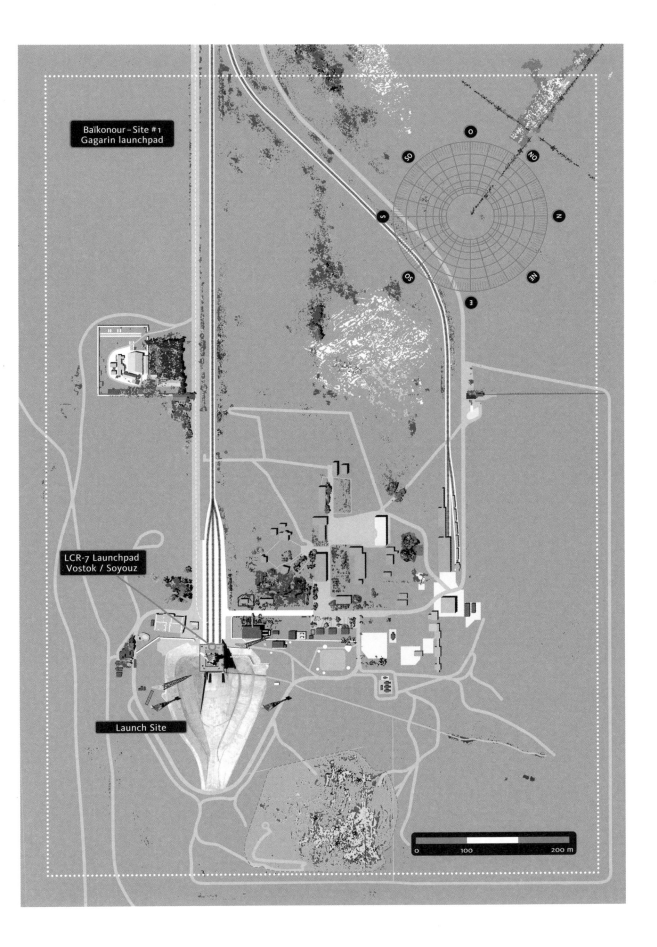

Baïkonour – Site #1
Gagarin launchpad

LCR-7 Launchpad
Vostok / Soyouz

Launch Site

O
SO
NO
S
N
SO
NE
E

0   100   200 m

Mont Rainier

Franconia

Bryn Athyn

Area 51

Hanover

Mountain View

Roswell

Nazca

THE AMERICAS

Varginha

Trindade

14° 43' 0" S, 75° 8' 0" W

THE PRE-COLUMBIAN LINES

NAZCA (PERU)

A desert littered with red stones, at the center of Peru: it is here that in 1927, the Peruvian archeologist Toribio Mejia Xesspe discovered strange furrows that could not directly be explained by agriculture. Carved into the gypseous soil, they appear as clear white lines on the stony ground, which owes its rusty-red color to its high iron oxide content. Someone has patiently piled up the red rocks along the edges to accentuate the contrast of these lines, each of which forms a giant figure, artfully traced, and clearly distinguishable only from the sky.

> One of the geoglyphs, however, looks so much like a humanoid being in a spacesuit that he was dubbed "the astronaut": his large, round eyes are focusing on the sky while he is sending an enigmatic greeting in that direction.

Seen from a plane, you can discern hundreds of geoglyphs—as these drawings on the ground are called—that are the legacy of the Nazcas, a pre-Inca people who inhabited the area between the third century BCE and the seventh century CE. There is an elegantly drawn 180-foot-tall (55 meter) monkey next to a 440-foot-wide (134 meter) condor, a jaguar, a whale, and a gigantic spider surrounded by abstract symbols, neither of which indicates their meaning or possible use. Was it an irrigation system? A mythological pantheon? A ritualistic mercy seat similar to the rock paintings also practiced in the area? The silent prayer of the ancient Nazcas lends itself to all sorts of interpretations.

"Seen from the air, the clear-cut impression that the 37-mile-long plain of Nazca made on me was that of an airfield!" writes Erich von Däniken in *Chariots of the Gods* (translated by Michael Heron) in 1968–1969. "What is wrong with the idea that the lines were laid out to say to the 'gods': 'Land here! Everything has been prepared as 'you' ordered'?"

This thesis has been rejected by German researcher Maria Reiche, who spent her life surveying the reliefs in the desolate Nazca desert to study and measure these incomprehensible works that a forgotten people arduously carved in the soil. She argues that they constitute an astronomical calendar, dotted with zodiac signs. And it is wrong to say that you can see these drawings only from aboard an aircraft: you can also make them out from neighboring hilltops. When UNESCO added the Nazca lines to their World Heritage Sites in 1994, extraterrestrial interpretations did not play a part in the listing.

One of the geoglyphs, however, looks so much like a humanoid being in a spacesuit that he was dubbed "the astronaut": his large, round eyes are focusing on the sky while he is sending an enigmatic greeting in that direction.

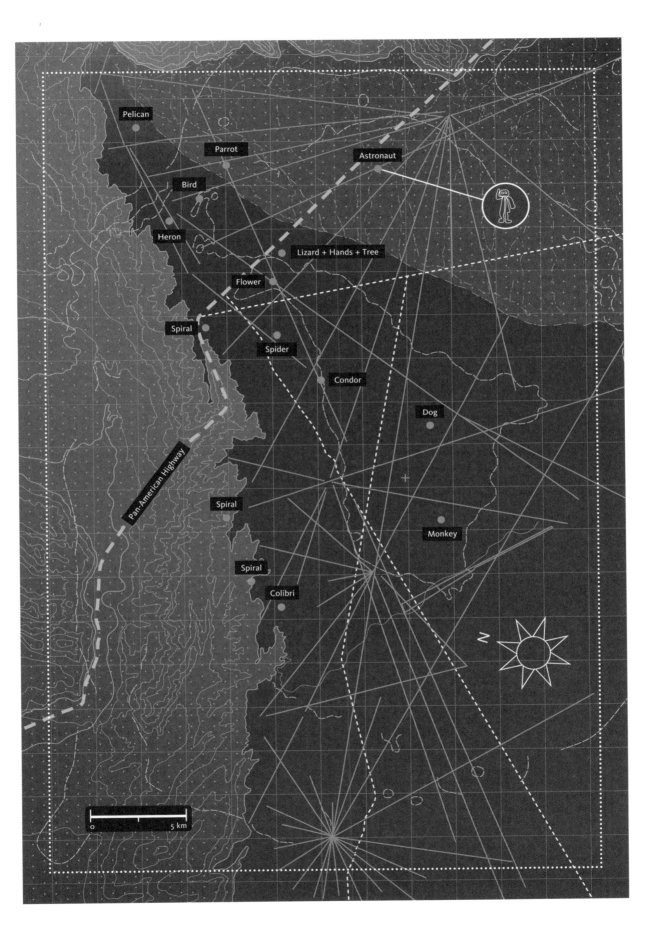

Pelican

Parrot

Bird

Astronaut

Heron

Lizard + Hands + Tree

Flower

Spiral

Spider

Condor

Dog

Pan-American Highway

Spiral

Monkey

Spiral

Colibri

N

0   5 km

40° 7' 53" N, 75° 4' 2" W

THE ASTRAL CHURCH

BRYN ATHYN (PENNSYLVANIA, UNITED STATES)

What if other planets were simply populated by earthmen and women? Or, at least, by human beings that are identical to us, because they stem from the same process of creation? That was Emanuel Swedenborg's wager, who referred to sacred Christian texts and tried to reason as logically as possible: "He who believes, as every one ought to believe, that the Deity created the universe for no other end than the existence of the human race, and of heaven from it (for the human race is the seminary of heaven), must also believe that wherever there is an earth, there are human inhabitants," he explained in 1758 in a most amazing book, translated as *Earths in the Universe* in 1860, which recounts his spiritual journeys through space.

If God is infinite, indeed, why would he have been so stingy as to populate a single planet? "What would this be to the Divine Being, who is infinite, and to whom thousands, nay myriads of earths, all filled with inhabitants, would be but a little thing and almost nothing!" he argues, before moving on to describe a multitude of celestial societies.

Born in Stockholm on January 29, 1688, to a very pious family, Swedenborg was first and foremost a scientist and an inventor, who, at the age of twenty-six, had already traveled to Europe's big cities to meet such enlightened minds as Newton, Leibniz, and Halley. The "Leonardo da Vinci of the North" drew plans for a steam engine, a propeller-driven spacecraft,

and a submarine before tackling algebra, physics, and the origins of the universe. He was interested in atoms, magnetism, and electricity, but this man of the Enlightenment would embark on even-more-dizzying mental exploits after the death of his father.

From 1744 onward, he had visionary dreams, met Jesus Christ, visited Paradise and Hell . . . Through the mercy of God, he explains, "the interiors which are of my spirit are opened in me," which allowed him to communicate mentally with other spirits in the vast universe. It is thus that he explored Mercury, Mars, and Saturn, and all the planets of the macrocosm forming the "Grand Man" in which humans are but microcosmic atoms.

> He who believes must also believe that wherever there is an earth, there are human inhabitants.

"Hence I could see that the speech of the inhabitants of Mars is different from that of the inhabitants of our earth. It is not sonorous, but almost tacit, entering the interior hearing and sight by a shorter way; consequently, it is more perfect and fuller of the ideas of thought, thus approaching nearer to the speech of spirits and angels," he confided after having been initiated in the mysterious cosmogonies by his Martian interlocutors who animate the brain for the "Grand Man."

"I observed a flaming object exceedingly beautiful; it was of various colors, purple and also

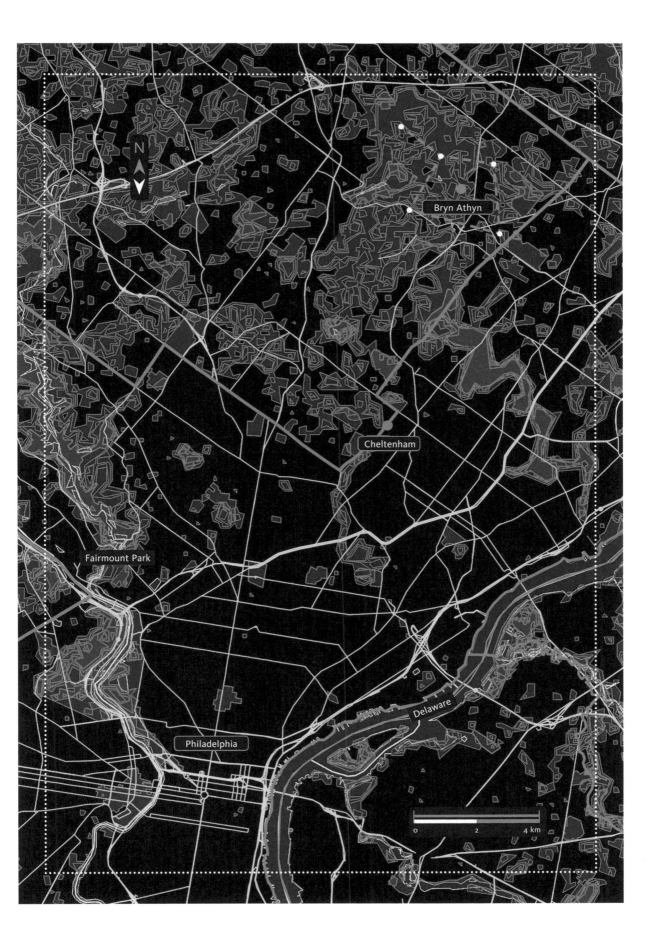

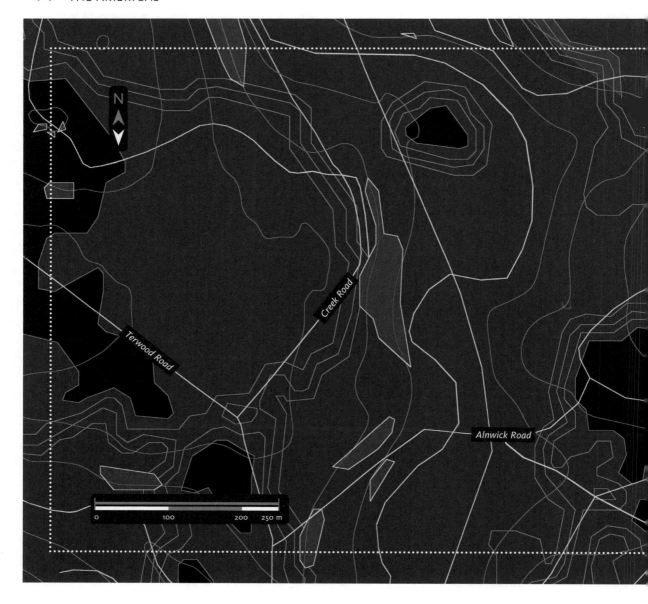

pale red, and from the flame the colors shone beautifully. I saw also the resemblance of a hand, to which the flame adhered," goes Swedenborg's witness account. A little later, he made out a firebird, the symbol of "celestial love," in this supernatural environment. The master died in London on March 29, 1772, before finishing the notation of his visions, but his disciples continued to read them with passion, especially since they discovered several unpublished volumes of *Arcana* *Cœlestia* and notes on *Apocalypse Revealed* among his estate. On the basis of these newly revealed texts, a Swedenborgian Church was founded in 1782 and soon spread to America.

Without insistent pushes to convert, this syncretic "New Church" still manages to find new disciples. Officially renamed "the New Church" in 1982, this Swedenborgian confession still exists today and counts thirty-five thousand believers on planet Earth alone.

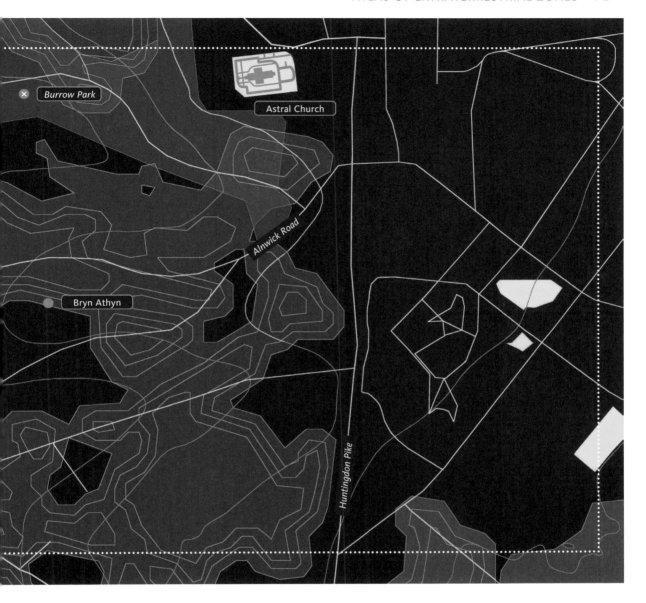

It is organized into national self-governing churches, the largest of which are located in the United States and South Africa, with its spiritual center in the small town of Bryn Athyn, Pennsylvania, close to Philadelphia. In this New Jerusalem of cosmic Christianity, friends of the angelic spirits from Mars can read about them at the Emanuel Swedenborg Library, enroll their children in the denominational college, or, on a nearby hill, admire the impressive cathedral that dominates Pennypack Creek valley. Built between 1913 and 1919 and completed with its Ezekiel Tower in the 1920s, the enormous building combines neo-Gothic architecture with elements reminiscent of Insular art.

Swedenborgians around the world can book their wedding slot online, and everyone else can simply visit and try to converse in spirit with the man who became known as a "close friend of the angels."

39° 11' 43" N, 76° 43' 22" W

THE INTERNATIONAL FORTEAN ORGANIZATION

HANOVER (MARYLAND, UNITED STATES)

A procession of the damned," Charles Fort promised his readers after his tireless work at the New York Library: "Battalions of the accursed, captained by pallid data that I have exhumed, will march.... Some of them livid and some of them fiery and some of them rotten," he predicted.

A ufologist (without being aware of it), Charles Hoy Fort was born in Albany on August 9, 1874. A journalist turned taxidermist, he sat in his shabby apartment in the Bronx compiling a tremendous dossier of unexplained phenomena he discovered in his readings. This fanatic compiler scoured newspapers and old books to find reports about raining frogs and meteorites, unknown materials washed up on beaches, falling clinker, and disappearances without a cause. In boxes piling up all over his home, this private detective of the supernatural amassed around twenty-five thousand fact sheets, packed with information on circumstances and details.

Then, in order to surpass this draft stage, he decided to burn the vast amount of documents to liberate himself from them, and to gain a wider, more general understanding based on new and even more numerous charts and sheets. This resulted in the publication of *The Book of the Damned* in 1919, a monument of intellectual dissent and the bible of speculative parascience.

"One of literature's monstrosities" writer Edmund Pearson judged it, yet this mad work and its 1923 sequel, *New Lands*, found many enthusiastic readers: "Reading Charles Fort is a ride on a comet," the thinker Maynard Shipley stated somewhat accurately.

In his writing, Charles Fort reshuffles the cards dealt by knowledge: the most fundamental of truths lapse into the uncertain, while an avalanche of "accursed facts," renounced by professors and the academies but revived by him, radically reverse the common point of view. "They are fishing for us," he suggested.... According to Fort, the earth is like a sinking ship in the ocean: it is cruising through space, as if it were lost in a "Super-Sargasso Sea," crossing paths with the wreckage of other worlds, deep-sea life-forms, and the incomprehensible manifestations of a distant otherness.

Reading Charles Fort is a ride on a comet.

"My own acceptance is that either a world or a vast super-construction . . . hovered over India in the summer of 1860," he wrote in a chapter on flying spacecrafts of unknown origin. "And, in the evening of this same day that something—took a shot at Dhurmsalla—or sent objects upon which there may be decipherable markings—lights were seen in the air— I think, myself, of a number of things, beings, whatever they were, trying to get down, but resisted, like balloonists, at a certain altitude, trying to get farther up, but resisted."

In Lebanon, Connecticut, "two triangular, luminous appearances" were recorded on the "evening of July 3, 1882, on the moon's upper

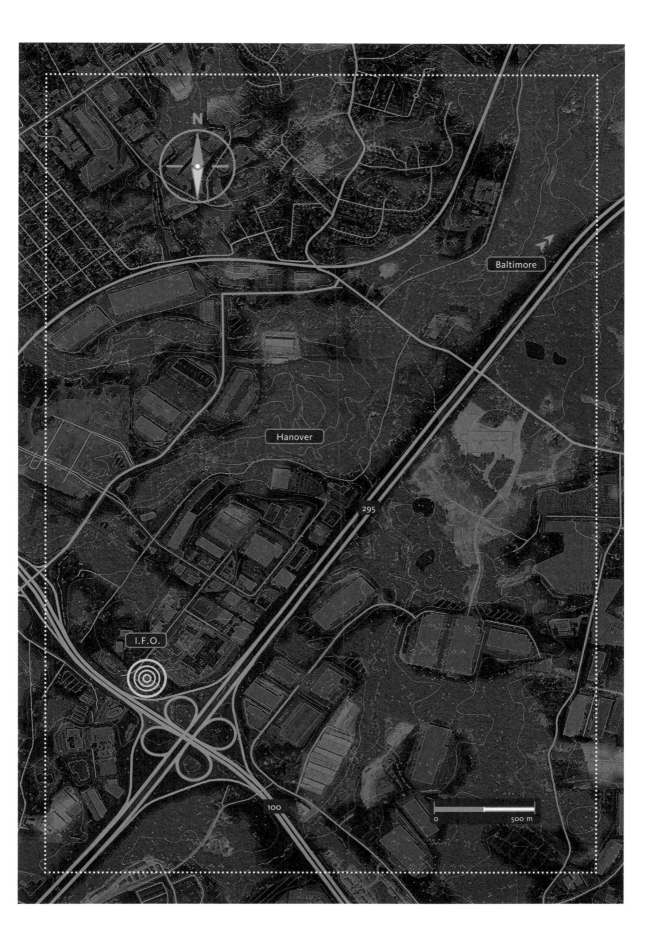

limb. They disappeared, and two dark triangular appearances . . . were seen three minutes later upon the lower limb. They approached each other, met, and instantly disappeared."

In England, "two stationary dark patches upon clouds" were reported by a witness on April 8, 1912, "rapidly moving. They were fan-shaped— or triangular—and varied in size." It was a "heavy shadow cast upon a thin veil of clouds by some unseen object away in the west, which was

intercepting the sun's rays." And this is how he goes on, over hundreds of pages . . . just like he promised in his jerky language: "The naïve and the pedantic and the bizarre and the grotesque and the sincere and the insincere, the profound and the puerile. A stab and a laugh and the patiently folded hands of hopeless propriety."

In 1931, when Charles Fort had only one year left to live, the aging autodidact was pleased to see the foundation of the Fortean Society, with the aim

of continuing his teachings. Among its founders were his friend the writer Theodore Dreiser, the psychologist Havelock Ellis, and the British novelist John Cowper Powys. The association has moved headquarters and changed its name several times; it nearly dissolved in 1959, after the death of its secretary-general Tiffany Thayer, but was reborn in the early 1960s under a meaningful acronym: INFO (International Fortean Organization). Based now in Hanover, Maryland, its journals, literature,

and conference center attract researchers specializing in the strange from around the world. They can get an annual membership for twenty-five dollars or become lifetime members for 250 dollars. Among them are ufologists, but also scientists and science fiction writers.

Charles Fort had a premonition this might happen: "Perhaps I am the pioneer of a future literature whose traitors and heroes will be tidal waves and stars, scarabs and earthquakes."

46° 51' 8" N, 121° 45' 37" W

THE FIRST FLYING SAUCERS

MOUNT RAINIER (WASHINGTON, UNITED STATES)

If only Mount Rainier could speak! At an altitude of 14,417 feet (4,392 meters), this squat volcano dominates the snow-covered backdrop to the cities of Tacoma and Seattle, Washington State, in the Pacific Northwest. It witnessed an important meeting—and everything we know about it, we were told by the then-thirty-five-year-old businessman Kenneth Arnold from Minnesota.

On June 24, 1947, Kenneth Arnold crossed the Cascade Range aboard his private single-engine plane, a small CallAir A-2 whose propeller spiraled through the air. He was on his way from Chehalis to Yakima, and, skirting around Mount Rainier, he suddenly crossed paths with an unlikely squadron: nine spacecrafts of an unusual shape, with an irregular flight pattern, moved through the air at a dizzying speed—possibly twice as fast as his plane!

When he landed in Yakima, Kenneth Arnold told a few pilot friends about the phenomenon. He then bravely took to the skies again, this time without noting anything abnormal, and got to Pendleton, in the neighboring state of Oregon.

There, he tried to get in touch with the FBI, though without success. At that point, Kenneth Arnold was mostly thinking of alerting them to a possible Soviet intrusion, not yet contemplating the hypothesis of aliens. Unable to alert the counterespionage services directly, he turned to the local media and knocked on the doors of the *East Oregonian*—that is how a little-known provincial newspaper became the first to hear of the extraordinary event, of the arrival in American airspace of crafts that, in the witness's own words, were "flying like saucers skipping across the water".

The two journalists dealing with his case, since they had not much else to do, also wrote a news dispatch for Associated Press—a dispatch that would instantly be disseminated across national and international networks. In a matter of days, the whole world was talking about the "flying saucers" of Mount Rainier, which numerous witnesses confirmed to have seen in various places. A rumor spread that was impossible to contain.

> Nine spacecrafts of an unusual shape moved through the air at a dizzying speed.

For his part, Kenneth Arnold would seek to correct what he was purported to have said. In particular, that the spacecrafts were flying "like saucers" but did not resemble them in shape: they were rounded at the front and pointed at the ends and looked more like croissants—which is what made skeptics suggest he had just encountered a pod of pelicans . . .

An illustrated pamphlet turned Kenneth Arnold into the first modern ufologist, the butt of "pelicanists." He died in Bellevue on January 16, 1984, not far from Mount Rainier, which jealously kept its secret. A previous apparition of saucers was reported here in 1947, and Kenneth Arnold tried to establish a link between the two observations. The two military personnel who accompanied him on his investigation were killed on their return flight, when their airplane crashed—which would forever give credence to conspiracy theories.

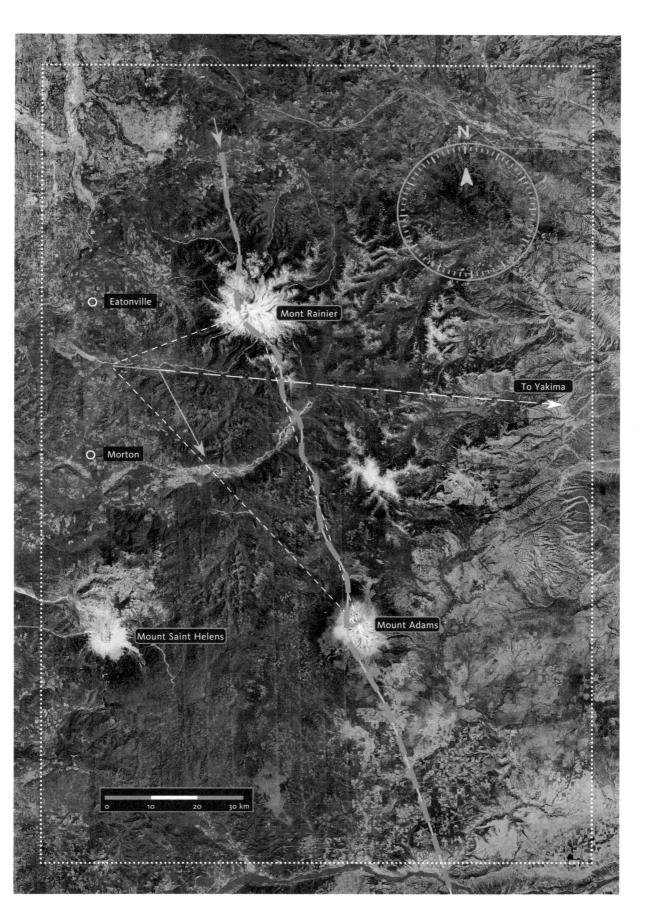

N

Eatonville

Mont Rainier

To Yakima

Morton

Mount Saint Helens

Mount Adams

0   10   20   30 km

33° 23' 39" N, 104° 31' 22" W

THE TWO CRASH SITES

ROSWELL (NEW MEXICO, UNITED STATES)

Of all the locations of encounters between humans and aliens, Roswell is by far the most famous. It is now impossible not to know that in July 1947, the crash of a flying saucer here in New Mexico turned into a state secret. And the discovery of a movie by the British producer Ray Santilli in 1995 provided the world with images of the official dissection of a six-fingered alien who died in the accident.

However, the case received little publicity at the time: beginning in 1950, ufologists managed to piece together what had happened, on the basis of leaked witness accounts. And the story is so convoluted that it involves not one but two sites in Roswell.

The first is the "debris site": here, 81 miles (130 kilometers) northwest of the town of Roswell, rancher William "Mac" Brazel discovered the metal fragments of an unidentified craft in his field on July 8, 1947. This gave rise to a bold press release by Colonel Blanchard, commander of the Roswell Air Force Base, announcing the crash of a "disc." The US Air Force headquarters in Fort Worth, Texas, immediately retracted the statement, stating that the brave rancher Mac had found nothing but the remains of a weather balloon . . .

It was on a second site, at a highly controversial location, that the wounded or killed aliens had apparently crashed to the ground and had been disappeared by the army—at the same time as Brazel came across the debris. Even if the balloon was related to Project Mogul—that is, if it was a surveillance balloon being tested for use

above the Soviet Union—the military's precautions lend credulity to the alien hypothesis, since their measures have been attributed to MJ-12, the secret service of the "Men in Black." Both the abundant literature that analyzes the circumstances of the crash and the events of 1947 that happened immediately after Kenneth Arnold's sightings on Mount Rainier, and the geopolitical repercussions of the case would let the imagination of prolific writers run wild.

> The military's precautions lent further credulity to the alien hypothesis.

The hypothesis that contact was made with the ufonauts before their death, or with aliens via the equipment found in the debris of the machine, now fuels the most elaborate of conspiracy theories. For some, the US has forged an alliance with exocivilizations, which would explain its technological advance over the Eastern Bloc. For others, the entire Cold War was a deception of the people: the United States and the USSR, in the guise of preparing for a nuclear conflict that would never happen, were jointly accumulating massive stockpiles of weapons to prepare for an alien invasion . . .

Yet another theory is that the crash was voluntarily orchestrated: altruistic aliens wanted to scare the inhabitants of the earth into joining forces, rather than killing each other . . . Grays are said to be great manipulators.

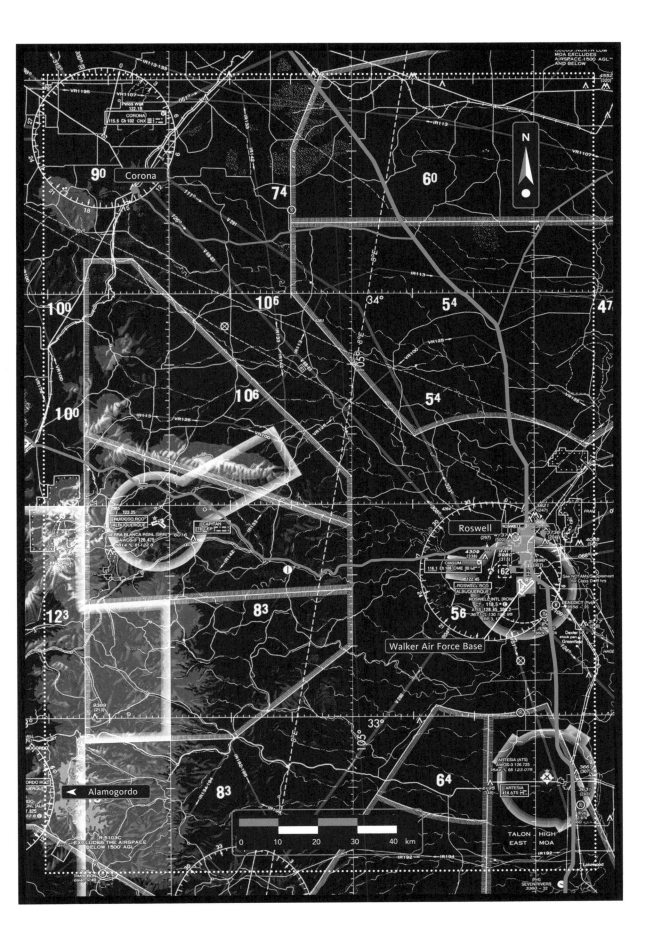

43° 54' 28" N, 71° 40' 2" W

THE ABDUCTION OF BARNEY AND BETTY HILL

FRANCONIA (NEW HAMPSHIRE, UNITED STATES)

On the night of September 19 to September 20, 1961, driving in their old Chevrolet Bel Air, Mr. and Mrs. Hill were returning from vacation. They had visited Quebec, had seen the Niagara Falls, and were on their way home to Portsmouth, New Hampshire. A close-knit, loving couple, free from prejudice: Betty is white and married to Barney, who is a post office employee, and Black. Both were beginning to find the journey a little tiring. It was about 10:30 p.m., when, south of Lancaster, they made out a glow that they first mistook for a shooting star, then for a passenger plane. When they got onto the Franconia Notch pass, they realized that a spacecraft bathed in light was swooping in on them. Barney had a pistol with him, but in the cataleptic state he and Betty soon found themselves in, he did not use it. When the Hills regained consciousness the following day, their car was 35 miles (56 kilometers) south of the place where they had been captured.

> In 1964, the couple took part in hypnosis experiments to recover more details.

At least, that is what Betty Hill told the Air Force and the ufologist Donald E. Keyhoe, who got the story out. This is the first public report of an "abduction"; that is, a kidnapping of earthlings by aliens with the aim of a biological examination. The scenario would often be repeated later, and each time the "abductees" would not recall the details, as if their persecutors had erased the event from their memory.

A few days later, however, anxious dreams enabled Betty to re-create the events of that crazy night: she recalled her abduction by small humanoid aliens that were organized like the military: a leader who interrogated her in English and sought to tranquilize her, and an unperturbed scientist who examined her and took hair samples, a nail fragment, and a swab of her skin.

In 1964, the couple took part in hypnosis experiments to recover more details. In 1966, a written account of the story hit the bookstores: *Interrupted Journey*, written by John G. Fuller. The author had interviewed the Hills and reproduced a map of the stars as seen from the aircraft and sketched by Betty. This map allowed a teacher and keen astronomer, Marjorie Fish, to locate that the Hills had been kidnapped by residents of Zeta Reticuli, a double-star system located 39 light-years away from Earth.

Lie, auto-suggestion, or hallucinatory delirium? Or was it a mixed-race couple's need for recognition in still-segregated America? Widowed in 1969, Betty Hill would affirm until her death on October 17, 2004, the truthfulness of her abduction by Zeta Reticulans. And the few motorists who spent the evening passing through the Franconia Notch, south of Lancaster, have felt a little tense ever since.

Lancaster

US 3

Carroll

Franconia

Mount Cannon

Lincoln

Tripoli Road

×

Mill Brook Road

Thornton

Campton

NH-175

Plymouth

Ashland

To Concord / Portsmouth

N
S

0   5 km

20° 30' 34" S, 29° 19' 32" W

THE UFO ISLAND

TRINDADE (BRAZIL)

In the middle of the ocean, Trindade Island is one of the most remote places in the world—alongside St. Helena and Tristan da Cunha, its far removed cousins in the South Atlantic Ocean.

Since it was still uninhabited in 1890, it sparked the ambition of adventurer James Harden-Hickey, who tried—unsuccessfully—to be recognized as its sovereign prince, calling himself James I. The British set up a coal depot here, prompting Brazil, in 1896, to assert its rights to this rocky goat-infested island of just 3.9 square miles (10 square kilometers) to prevent it from being annexed.

> A flying object rose from the horizon and seemed to park on the island's ridge for a moment; it then flew over the crew in a threatening way before disappearing in a flash.

In 1957, in preparation for the International Geophysical Year, the Brazilian navy dispatched a team of military and scientific personnel to conduct surveys. On January 16, 1958, the expedition was about to return on the tall ship *Almirante Saldanha* when a flying object rose from the horizon and seemed to park on the island's ridge for a moment; it then flew over the crew in a threatening way before disappearing in a flash. Forty-eight civilians and military

personnel were on deck and saw the saucer, yet the incident would never have been believed had it not been for Almiro Barauna, the professional photographer on board, who managed to take four snaps of the spacecraft.

Despite the cloudy sky, the evidence was so compelling that Brazil's president, Joscelino Kubitschek, authorized the publication of these snapshots in the press—the UFO soon featured on the front page of leading newspapers in Brazil and elsewhere. "It didn't seem to make a noise, although, given the screams of the people on deck, and the noise of the sea, I cannot be fully certain. It looked metallic, the color of ash, and there was something like green condensation vapor around its edges, especially toward the front. It moved in waves, like the flight of a bat," recalled Barauna, the star of the moment.

The investigation sowed discord, however, since it uncovered that four years earlier, the very same Barauna had shown how to doctor photos of UFOs, proving this event was a hoax. His work on "debunking"—to use the terminology of ufologists—might have given him hope of fame and glory. Could it be that the expert himself had become a hoaxer, or did the debunker get caught in his own trap?

Since 1957, Trindade has been guarded by some thirty sailors, who are the only inhabitants of the island: a possible return of the UFO would therefore fall within the remit of military secrets.

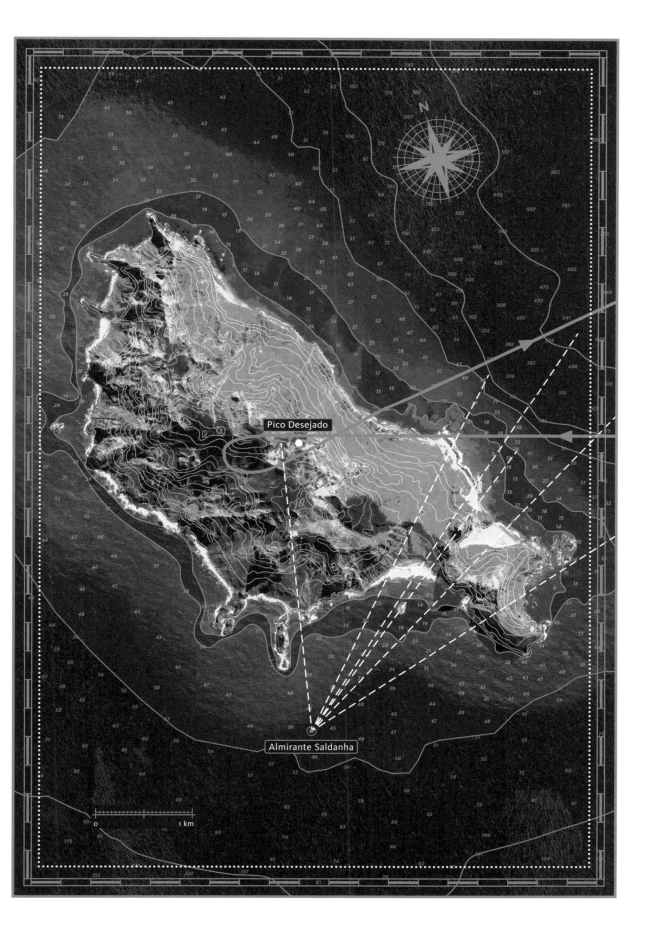

Pico Desejado

Almirante Saldanha

N

0   1 km

21° 33' 21" S, 45° 26' 12" W

THE WOUNDED DEVIL

VARGINHA (BRAZIL)

Life had been quiet in Varginha, in the Brazilian state of Minas Gerais, when the events of January 20, 1996, turned the provincial city of one hundred twenty thousand inhabitants, known until then for the quality of its coffee, into the "Brazilian Roswell."

On that day, in the late afternoon, Valquiria Fatima Silva, her sister Liliane, and their friend Katia Andrade Xavier were on their way home after a day at work. The three young women were tired and decided to take a shortcut through an unoccupied subdivision—which is where they had the fright of their lives: stretched out along the wall was a naked creature with brown, smooth and sticky skin; red eyes; and three large protuberances on its bombastic skull, which the women thought to be the horns of a devil. The demon seemed very much exhausted, the way it was lying there. They ran as fast as their legs would carry them, and alerted their families and friends.

When the mother of the two sisters, accompanied by a neighbor, arrived at the indicated place, the creature had disappeared, but bloodstains so dark they were almost black and smelled dreadful indicated that an injured being must indeed have paused at the spot. From then on, an obsessive fear took over the city, and it became difficult to distinguish eyewitness accounts from rumors: the Brazilian army pretended to have organized a hunt to capture the creature and perhaps its fellow travelers; a farmer saw soldiers remove saucer debris and whisk it away; covered trucks had sped the wreckage away to a secret base, all the while at least one alien had undergone autopsy at Campinas University Hospital; and one of the military police officers engaged in the operation, a strong and healthy man, is said to have wasted away after having been in contact with the space travelers involved in the accident.

> Stretched out along the wall was a naked creature with brown, smooth and sticky skin; red eyes; and three large protuberances on its bombastic skull, which the women thought to be the horns of a devil.

As in Roswell, the Brazilian authorities' denials only aroused further suspicion and curiosity: the city of Varginha has since become a tourist attraction and cultivates the story. It has even erected a water tower in the shape of a spaceship in the middle of a crossroads. At the top of a high column, and illuminated at night, the concrete UFO also serves as a lighthouse for ufonauts, to prevent another crash.

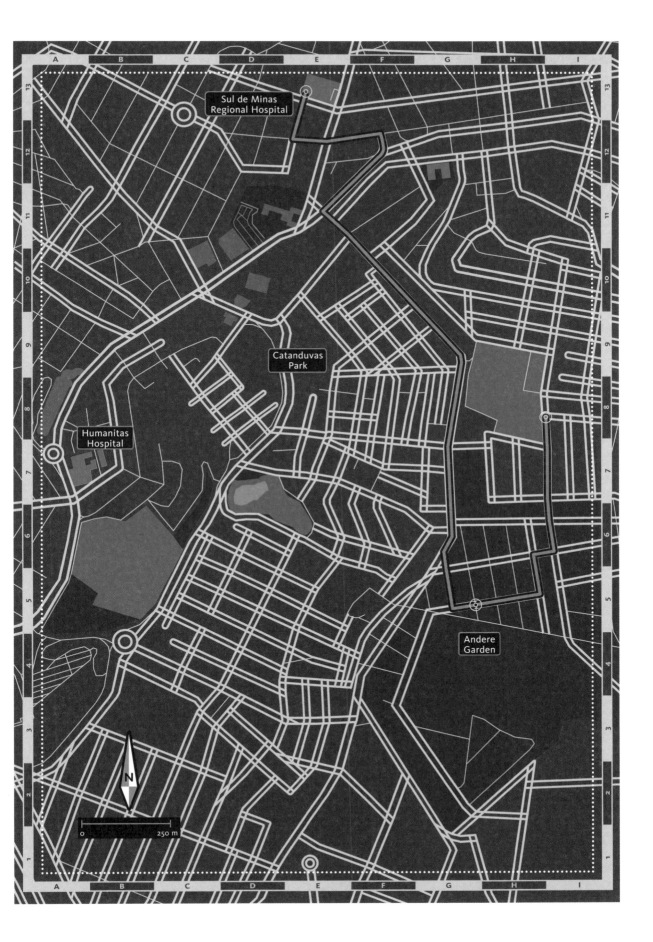

Sul de Minas
Regional Hospital

Catanduvas
Park

Humanitas
Hospital

Andere
Garden

N

0   250 m

37° 14' 6" N, 115° 48' 40" W

WELCOME TO DREAMLAND

AREA 51 (NEVADA, UNITED STATES)

Area 51 truly exists: it is part of a vast US Air Force base that was previously secret but has been officially recognized since 1995. In the middle of the Nevada desert, it spans 139 square miles (360 square kilometers), making it larger than several sovereign microstates, such as Grenada and Malta.

What remains shrouded in mystery is the activity that takes place there. Are they testing prototypes, like in the good old days of the Cold War and the Lockheed U-2 reconnaissance aircraft? Are they still dissembling other nations' machines here, such as Russian MiGs redirected to the West to undergo close scrutiny? A persistent rumor has it that you could find a model of every type of warplane used worldwide here.

> The largest of these, the mythical Hangar No. 18, is said to house the debris of the crashed Roswell spacecraft, and even the bodies of its passengers.

But these notions are based on rational facts: the secret that enshrouds the base, the no-fly zone above it, its exemption from environmental laws—all these nurture the most outlandish of assumptions. Satellite photos of the area show runways, a control tower, its headquarters—in short: all typical airbase features—but also vast hangars with problematic content. The largest of these, the mythical Hangar No. 18, is said to house the debris of the

crashed Roswell spacecraft, and even the bodies of its passengers. In 1989, one Bob Lazar claimed to have worked on nine spacecrafts of extraterrestrial origin in Sector Four, close to Area 51. There is nothing to confirm his claims, not even his degree as an engineer—Lazar accuses the secret services of erasing all traces of his past.

Furthermore, Area 51 encompasses Groom Lake, the dried-out bed of a former lake. Wild conspiracy theories have it that the depths underneath the salt flats hide an underground base run by aliens: apparently, ever since the first contact made at Roswell, the US government has stuck to a pact with the invaders that consists of a cynical and thoroughly dishonorable deal. Against the technological advances that have so far guaranteed its hegemony, the White House is said to have allowed a secret alien colony to be established and to let the extraterrestrials take a quota of humans for its biological experiments . . .

The nickname given to the impenetrable Area 51, "Dreamland," somewhat makes sense. Just two hours from Las Vegas, this dreamland attracts fanatical conspiracy theorists but also curious observers, to the extent that the nearby village of Rachel lives largely by selling souvenirs and that State Route 375 has been declared the "Extraterrestrial Highway" by local authorities.

But Area 51 may just be a decoy: while tourists flock to the region, the secret world government may be quietly working away on its teleporting trials in the inaccessible Area 6113, in the most-remote parts of Alaska . . .

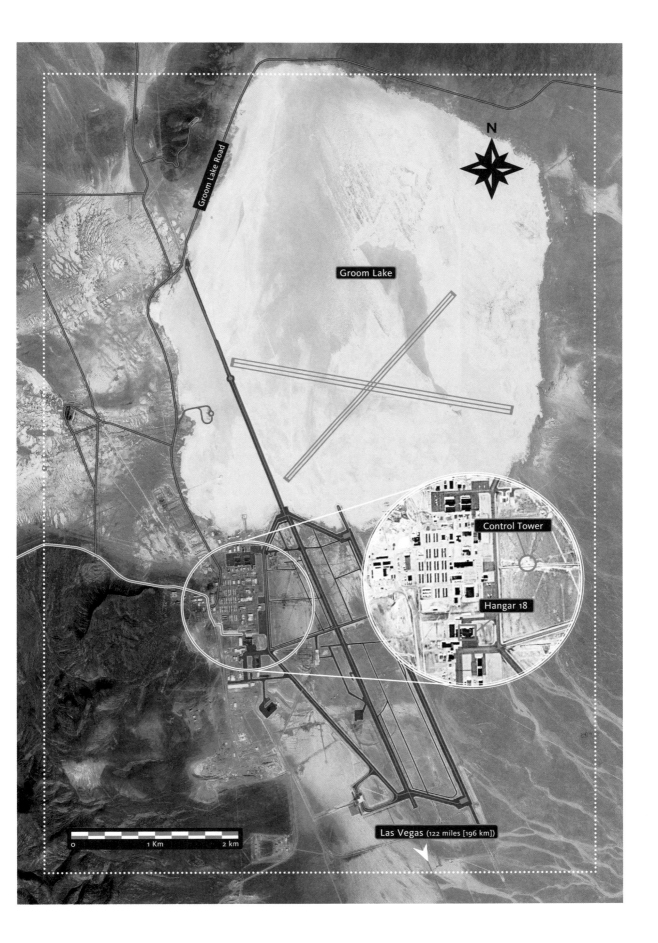

N

Groom Lake Road

Groom Lake

Control Tower

Hangar 18

Las Vegas (122 miles [196 km])

0   1 Km   2 km

37° 23' 10" N, 122° 3' 4" W

THE SETI INSTITUTE

MOUNTAIN VIEW (CALIFORNIA, UNITED STATES)

With its seventy-five thousand inhabitants, Mountain View is a neat small town south of San Francisco Bay, in Santa Clara County, California. Known for its Computer History Museum, it is located in the heart of Silicon Valley and, as its name suggests, offers an unobstructed view of its surroundings

> Statistically, it has become really quite difficult to think that we should be alone in the universe.

This bright place with its pleasant climate is not only home to "new economy" companies. Indeed, at 189 Bernardo Avenue, a chic building modeled on a Roman villa houses the headquarters of a not-for-profit organization that makes the world dream: the SETI Institute (which stands for "Search for Extraterrestrial Intelligence") was set up to "explore, understand, and explain the origin, nature, and prevalence of life in the universe."

In 1959, the American physicists Phil Morrison and Giuseppe Cocconi initiated research into locating radio and laser signals issued by exocivilizations. According to astrobiologist Nathalie Cabrol, head of the institute's Carl Sagan Center, this research remains the "Holy Grail" of the SETI Institute but she also explores other avenues. "Statistically, it has become really quite difficult to think that we should be alone in the universe," she told the French magazine *La Recherche* in November 2016, even though, she warned, "extraterrestrial life is unlikely to resemble us, especially if it is complex."

Hence the idea of studying the icy moons of giant planets such as Enceladus or Europa, the subsoil of telluric planets, and even biochemical clues that might be contained in the atmosphere of certain exoplanets.

The global network of radar observatories is complemented by ambitious programs with next-generation probes and flying telescopes that will expand useful data. Simultaneously, research continues into the very notions of life and communication between living beings that fall within the purview of both philosophy and science. If we ever get a hello from an extraterrestrial biological entity, Mountain View offices are sure to be the first ones to be notified.

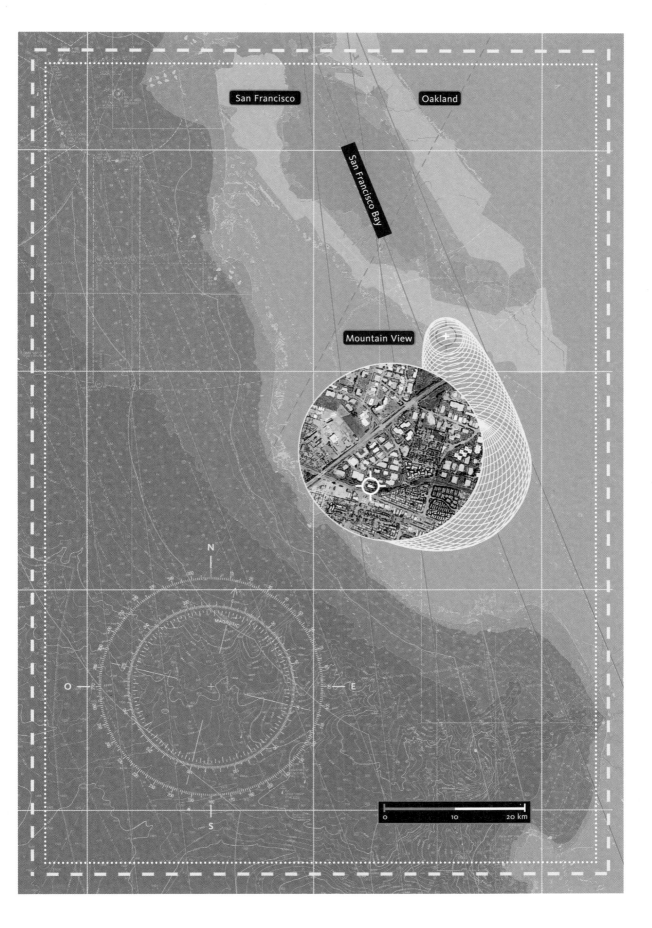

San Francisco

Oakland

San Francisco Bay

Mountain View

N

MAGNETIC

O

E

S

0   10   20 km

Pohnpei

OCEANIA

Parkes

06° 51' 0" N, 158° 13' 0" E

THE LOST CITY OF THE PACIFIC

POHNPEI (MICRONESIA)

Better than Easter Island and its large stone moais: Ponape Island is home to the remains of an entire city, Nan Madol, made up of black basalt blocks so large that one wonders what feat it took to get them here, so far from where they were quarried. Legend has it that two giant twins from the west conquered the island and levitated the stones to raise the city above the water, resting it on a coral reef and several artificial islets.

The uninhabited Nan Madol is today just a historical remnant of the past, visited by very few tourists who venture to the remote island, renamed Pohnpei, with the eponymous state being one of the four Federated States of Micronesia. Independent since 1990, Micronesia includes the Caroline Islands, which were formerly administered by the Americans, who had claimed them off the Japanese in 1944, who had previously taken them off the Germans in 1914, who had bought them, in 1899, from the Spanish, who, in turn, had been present there since the seventeenth century. Before all these invaders, however, a vibrant civilization had lived here, building a remote aquatic capital under the little-known Saudeleur dynasty.

This inexplicable city, in the middle of the Pacific Ocean, inspired two major science fiction and fantasy writers: first, Abraham Merritt, who wrote *The Moon Pool* in 1919, and after him H. P. Lovecraft, who based the sunken city of R'lyeh on it, where the "Great Old One," the Cthulhu, vegetates, a creature with an octopus-like head that other writers later picked up, creating a true Cthulhu cycle.

> Legend has it that two giant twins from the west conquered the island and levitated the stones to raise the city above the water.

Pohnpei is not unique as such, but its small population stands out because of a widespread substantial genetic anomaly that is extremely rare in the rest of the world: achromatopsia—that is, total color blindness. The island's isolation, a cause of inbreeding, may have fostered the transmission of this condition but it is unknown when and in what context the first cases appeared. Perhaps aliens were color-blind?

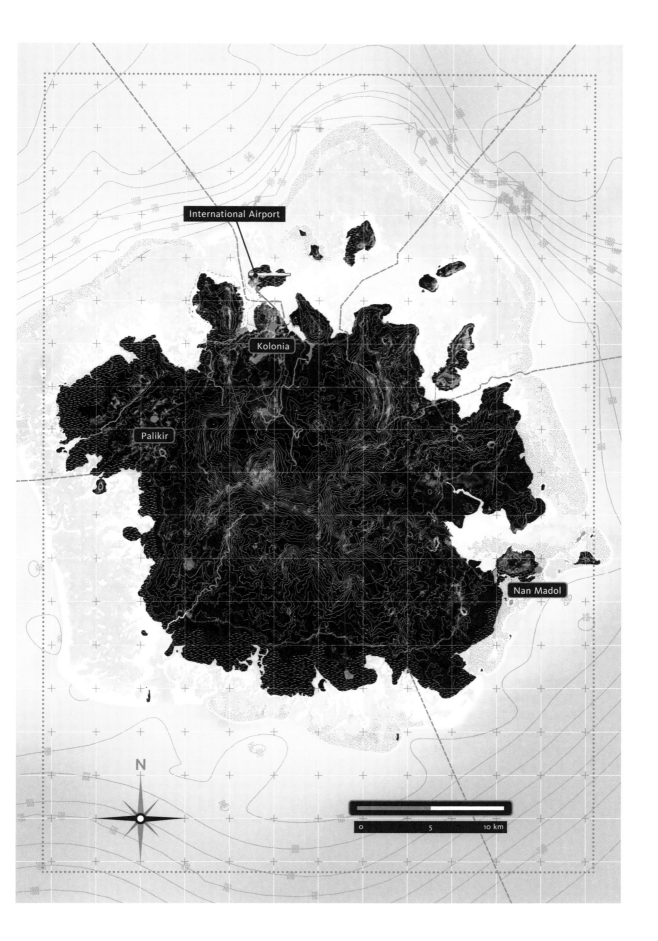

International Airport

Kolonia

Palikir

Nan Madol

N

0   5   10 km

33° 0' 0" S, 148° 15' 43" E

THE HOT WAVES

PARKES (AUSTRALIA)

The Parkes Observatory, 12.4 miles (20 kilometers) north of the small town of the same name, is located in the Australian state of New South Wales. Inaugurated in 1961, it entered the annals of space conquest eight years later, since—as a commemorative plaque on the building recalls—it was through this observatory that on July 21, 1969, images of the first steps on the moon were transmitted through the airwaves live onto TV screens worldwide. In addition to the Apollo missions, the observatory has tracked numerous space probes, thanks to its radio telescope: a flat, white, circular antenna and receiver with a diameter of 230 feet (70 meters), earning it the moniker "the Dish."

Since its inception, such equipment has contributed to the SETI program: its huge radio-astronomical ear spies on interstellar space, ready to pick up any messages or voluntary or involuntary signals that might be emitted by exocivilizations.

One early morning, after forty years of silence, a brief and intense surge was finally detected, in a band ranging from 2.3 to 2.5 gigahertz—no terrestrial experiment or any spatial phenomenon could explain it. It was a "monumental and cataclysmic" event, as described by the astrophysicist who headed the observation unit.

The Parkes team, eager to enter history for a second time, has recorded these mysterious "radio wave surges" for years, but scientists were wary. Over time, it appeared that most signals occurred only on weekdays during office hours—funny to think that there should be humdrum alien pen pushers who would respect weekends and nighttimes when their human counterparts were off work.

Equipped with an interference detector, the radio astronomers of Parkes finally grasped the sad facts: one of them, too eager to scoff his lunch, had developed the annoying habit of opening the microwave before it had pinged. While the microwave cycle would stop almost immediately when the door was opened, stray waves would escape each time and interfere with the nearby radio telescope. The captured waves did not come from Sirius or Alpha Centauri but from the cafeteria . . .

> Its huge radio-astronomical ear spies on interstellar space, ready to pick up any messages emitted by exocivilizations

This is an illustration that scientific evidence does not account for much if the protocol is not impeccably followed. The Dish that was tricked by its microwave: sounds like a fairy tale.

Yet, confirmed ufologists stress that the first observation, in 2001, took place very early in the day, at 5:50 a.m., that no one was heating up meals in the small hours, and that this laughable microwave story could be only a clever cover-up . . .

Alectown

Goobang National Park

Parkes Observatory

Radio Telescope

EW Track

N

0   1   2 km

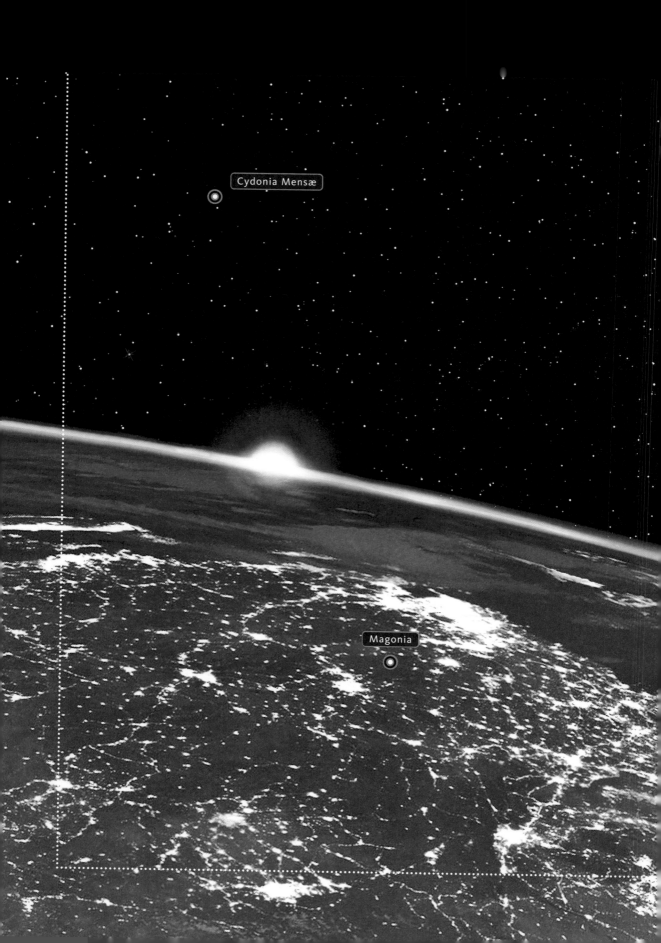

Cydonia Mensæ

Magonia

ELSEWHERE

New Swabia

Etheria

Thus, expressions of alien life have been recorded on every continent, in the mountains as well as in the plains, in cities, and in the middle of deserts. Specialist journals such as *Phénomènes spatiaux* or *Lumières dans la nuit* report thousands of more or less credible observations, encounters, abductions, crop circles, and geoglyphs—not to mention stories that cannot be mapped.

Ufologists speak only in hushed voices about the extraterrestrial colony of Etheria, whose location on Earth is kept secret, and some wonder whether it might not be confused with the moving or untraceable bases that are traditionally located in the clouds, in the water, or in the ice.

In the Middle Ages, so-called *tempestarii* were indeed thought to be located in the clouds and knew of the mobile lands of Magonia, from where they were able to unleash the elements: flying vessels operated a shuttle between this celestial state and its allies on Earth—until inquisitors burned the latter at the stake for witchcraft.

In the oceans, the myth of the Bermuda Triangle has long fueled fears of a submerged base that would make passing ships and planes disappear forever. Even earlier than that, sailors knew that they were at risk when nearing White Island, a cursed island from which no one escaped with a sane mind, that did not feature on any map, yet stories of which throughout the world's oceans are identical. "Night fell, as it does in these parts, suddenly," recounts a captain in the French weekly travel journal *Le Journal des voyages* from November 28, 1880, "and suddenly, the sea turned phosphorescent but obtained such phosphorescence that you may have said the ocean were on fire. The ship, from the top of the great mast to the sheet, from bow to stern, had the appearance of quicksilver. We ourselves were white as ghosts: every step we took sent out sparks." This story was penned by the writer Bénédict-Henry Révoil and took the form of fiction, but it is based on a well-known maritime disaster that closely resembles the observations made during the big waves of UFO sightings since 1947.

In the perpetual ice, there is another myth of popular culture, that of Nazis surviving in Antarctica. It is true that Hitler Germany claimed the vast part of the white continent that other powers had rejected. This remote province of the Third Reich was named New Swabia and was said to have hidden a secret base after 1945, a

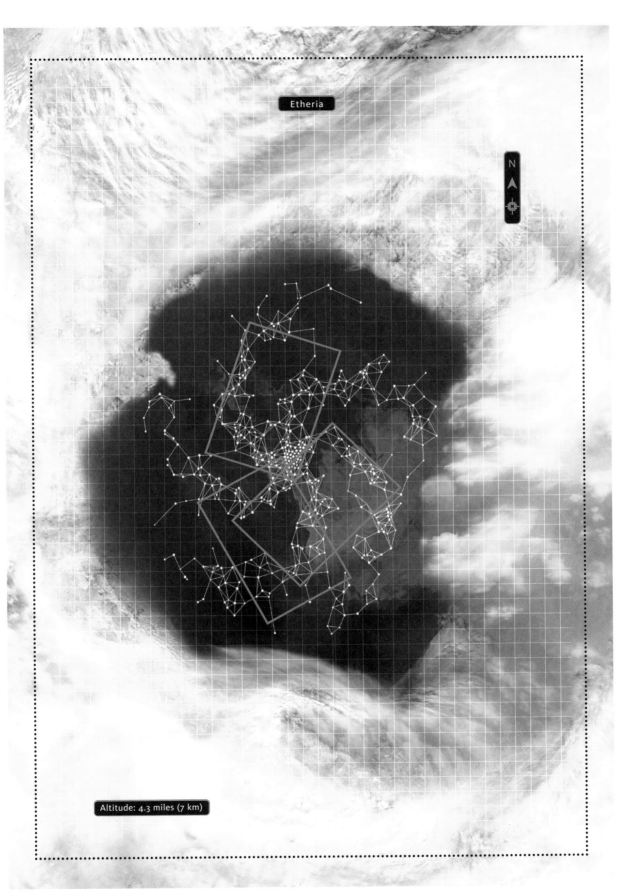

Etheria

Altitude: 4.3 miles (7 km)

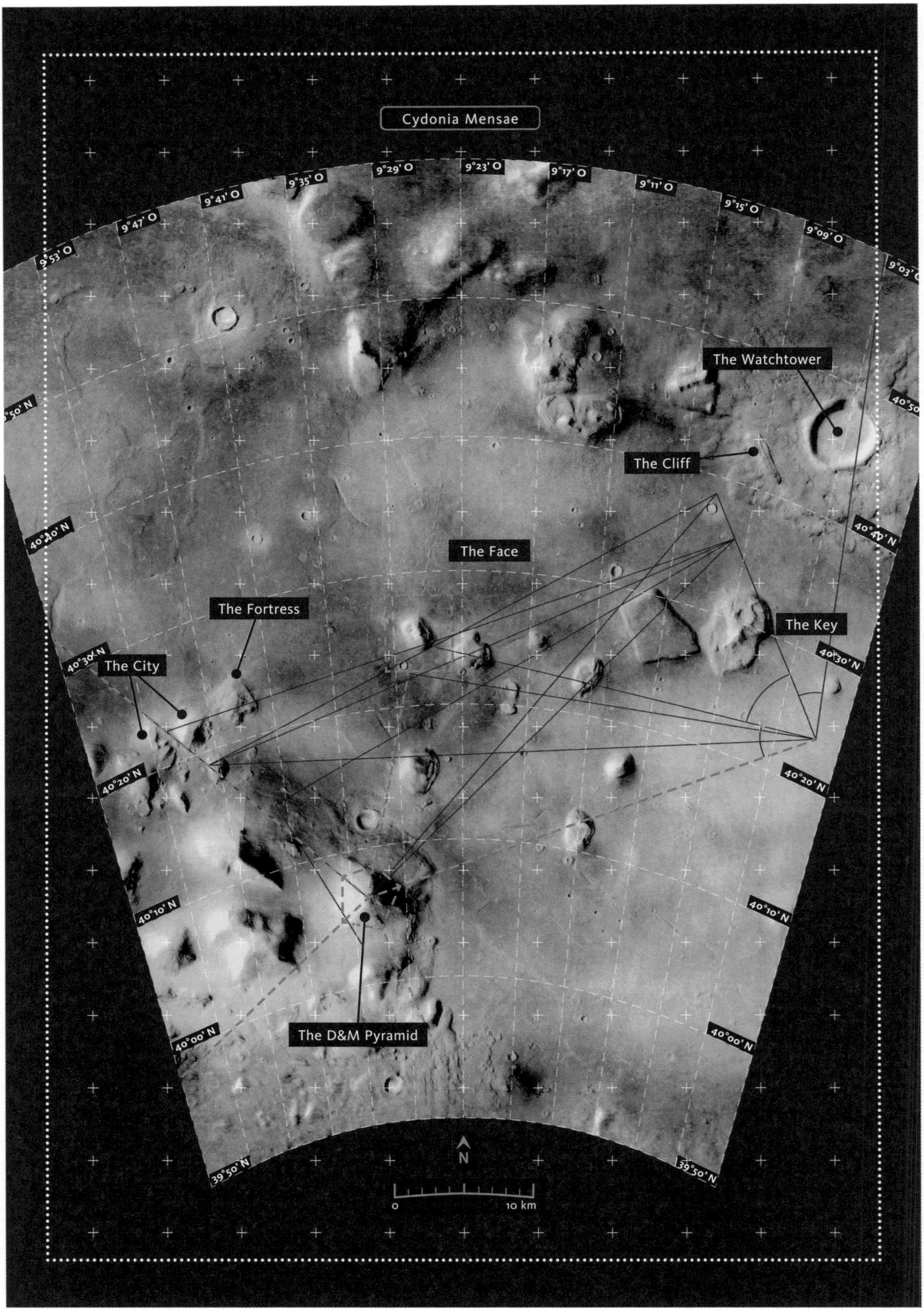
Cydonia Mensae
9°53' O
9°47' O
9°41' O
9°35' O
9°29' O
9°23' O
9°17' O
9°11' O
9°15' O
9°09' O
9°03' O
The Watchtower
The Cliff
The Face
The Fortress
The Key
The City
The D&M Pyramid
40°50' N
40°40' N
40°30' N
40°20' N
40°10' N
40°00' N
39°50' N
N
0
10 km

base connected with intraterrestrial peoples Hitler also believed in, or even with the Venusians or the Nordic aliens with whom the Nazis were seeking an alliance. The subject offers plenty of material for B movies, though it is hardly more or less believable than the Roswell follies in the powerful vortex of human imagination . . .

> On planet Mars, in an area known as Cydonia Mensæ, the Viking 1 orbiter photographed a unique face of stone on July 25, 1976.

Paradoxically, it is difficult to find traces of extraterrestrial civilizations in space: after having dreamed of Selenites for a long time, humans had to come to terms with the moon being uninhabited, as are all the other stars of the solar system, from what we know. If there is an exocivilization out there, it must be so far away that we cannot make it out or even understand it, despite the technological treasures of the SETI program. And it is doubtlessly because it manages to escape the desperate assessment of the Martian "Face of Cydonia" that has so seduced us earthlings.

On planet Mars, in an area known as Cydonia Mensæ, the Viking 1 orbiter photographed a unique face of stone on July 25, 1976, with a severe and oddly stupefied expression, lying on the ground like the vestige of an ancient civilization.

Is it an optical illusion, a whim of nature? Probably, but NASA's overly rational explanations only fueled the flames, and soon enough ufologists discovered pyramids, an ancient city, a geometric plan created by active intelligent life in the blurry images of the orbiter.

The woeful and friendly-looking "Face on Mars" seems to correspond to the Sphinxes of Egypt, the astronaut of Nazca, and the moais of Easter Island, in that it shows that humankind is definitely not alone in the universe.

Magonia

Altitude: 9.9 miles (16 km)

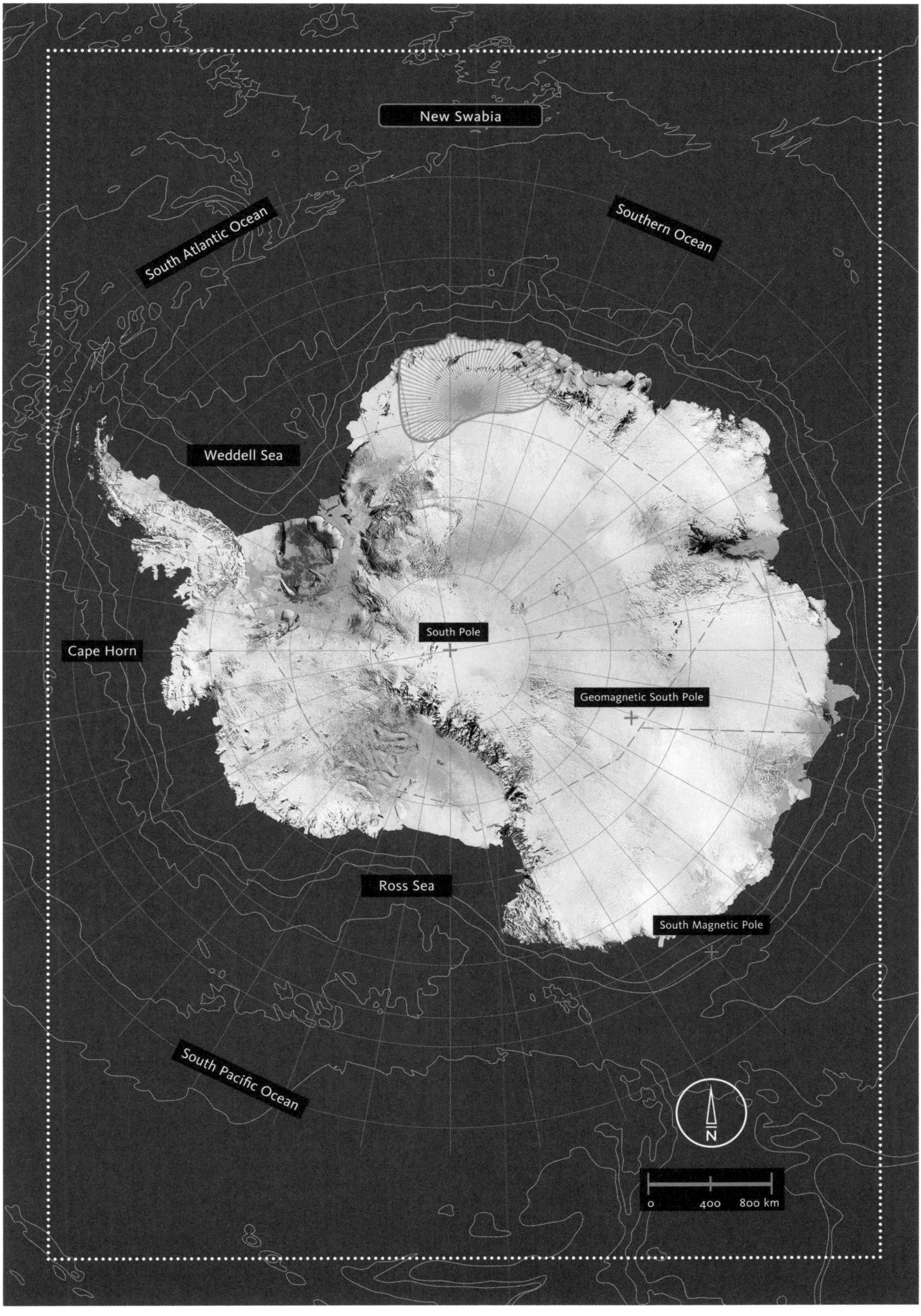

New Swabia

South Atlantic Ocean

Southern Ocean

Weddell Sea

Cape Horn

South Pole

Geomagnetic South Pole

Ross Sea

South Magnetic Pole

South Pacific Ocean

N

0   400   800 km

UFO GLOSSARY

A

abductee (n.): A human kidnapped by aliens

abduction (n.): The kidnapping of a human aboard a UFO*

albedo (n.): A Latin word for the reflectivity of an object (i.e., the relationship between absorbed and reflected light). Gas planets have a strong "albedo," unlike terrestrial planets.

ancient astronauts (locution [loc.]): Within the theory of history expressed by some ufologists* such as the Swiss Erich von Däniken, these are extraterrestrial visitors who came to planet Earth a very long time ago and whose memory is preserved in humanity's mythological and religious accounts. Human life itself could be seen as a creation by these original ufonauts*.

animal mutilations (loc.): Attacks on livestock as proof of an unknown carnivorous presence. Single animals or whole flocks can become victims of starving Dracos* or little-known creatures such as the chupacabras of Puerto Rico, a kind of vampiric predator whose name translates as "goat-sucker."

Annunaki (adj. and n.): In Mesopotamian scriptures, these designate the ruling class among the gods. According to theories of ancient astronauts,* these deities were of extraterrestrial origin and created humankind to serve them. The Annunaki were reportedly the first Reptilians* to have put foot on planet Earth.

Arcturian (adj. and n.): An alien of the "sixth density" (i.e., immaterial), from the red star of Arcturus, who communicates with earthlings by telepathy or channeling*.

B

Baal (adj. and n.): Alien species from the planet Baavi, with a secret base on planet Earth and a network of informants, according to the revelations of adventurer MNY (real name: Stephan Richer), founder of the Baal-Contact sect

Baavi'an (adj.): Related to the Baals* and their planet of origin, Baavi.

rods (n., pl.): Tiny, rudimentary shapes that appear on photographs or film. These can be rationally explained as interference caused by capturing insects in flight in front of the lens; some ufologists* interpret rods as manifestations of unknown life forms of extraterrestrial origin, comparable to the Xipéhuz*.

Blond (n.): An alien of human appearance, presenting as the Scandinavian type; these significantly differ from Grays* and Reptilians* in that they feature prominently in the esoteric ufology* of the Far Right. Extraterrestrial visitors are also called Talls* or Nordics*.

C

Cassiopeian (adj. and n.): An alien of the "sixth density" (i.e., immaterial), from the constellation of Cassiopeia, who communicates with earthlings by telepathy or channeling*

celeston (n.): An extraterrestrial currency brought into circulation by E. T. Mangan on behalf of the Nation of Celestial Space (Celestia). Subdivided into "joules" and "ergs," the celeston has taken the form of a tiny gold coin to minimize the cost of intergalactic transport.

channeler (n.): A human being used in the channeling* process

channeling (n.): Written or oral account of an immaterial entity that takes control of a living person to express itself. According to various esoteric traditions, deceased humans, supernatural beings, and divinities make their presence known in this way, and some extraterrestrials also use this technique, such as the Pleiadians*.

chemtrails (n., pl.): A term designating chemical contrails in the atmosphere. Conspiracy theorists assume these toxic clouds are of human origin, with the aim of weakening the people and making them dependent on their rulers, but some ufologists* consider them to be of extraterrestrial origin.

contactee (n.): A human being interacting with an extraterrestrial entity, either through direct contact or by telepathic communication or channeling*

cover-up (n.): From the related verb, referring to the concealment of an object or phenomenon by a government agency, such as the CIA or the MJ-12*

crop circle (n.): A pattern mysteriously drawn in a field, either on soft soil or in crops. These imprints usually form a circle and are often interpreted as evidence of a spaceship landing.

D

debunking (n.): A form of exposing a theory, a strategy of systematically discrediting any kind of testimonies concerning UFOs*

Devil's Department (loc.): Nickname given to a division of the former Soviet KGB specializing in collecting information on UFOs*, which were officially considered to be American spaceships flying over the USSR for espionage purposes. This is the Soviet, Cold War–era equivalent of the American MJ-12*.

Draco (n.): An apocopation of Draconian, this term refers to extraterrestrials of the Reptilian* type, with pointy, long teeth. Driven by malicious intentions, the "Dracos" or lizards* present on planet Earth are in hiding while waiting for reinforcements from Alpha Draconis to allow them to dominate our planet. For them, earthlings are a food resource.

E

EBE (abr.): Initialism for "extraterrestrial biological entity"

Elohim (n., pl.): One of the biblical names of God, believed by Raëlists* to refer to the inhabitants of the planet where their prophet Raël's revelation took place in 1975: these small humanoid aliens, with their pale-green skin and almond-shaped eyes, are said to have produced human DNA in laboratories 25,000 years ago, thus inspiring the figure of God, the creator of Jews and Christians. They are said to be preparing for their return to earth in 2025.

ETH (abr.): The initialism of "extraterrestrial hypothesis" (i.e., the boldest explanation for UFO* sightings)

exocivilization (n.): An extraterrestrial civilization

exolanguage (n.): An alien language, such as Martian taught by Hélène Smith

exoplanet (n.): A planet located outside the solar system

experiencer (n.): Derived from the word "experience," this term refers to a person who has experienced an extraterrestrial phenomenon, which can be either of a physical or spiritual nature.

F

flying cigar (loc.): A type of UFO* of oblong shape

flying disc (n.): A type of UFO* that is circular in shape, generally large in size, and repeatedly featured in witness accounts

foo fighter (loc.): A term designating aerial phenomena reported by Allied pilots at the end of World War II, which took the form of small fireballs of unknown origin

Fortean (adj.): Adjective relating to the American writer Charles Fort (1874–1932) and his work, in particular *The Book of the Damned*. A "Fortean phenomenon" is a paranormal event.

G

GEIPAN (abr.): The French abbreviation for the unidentified aerospace phenomenon research and information group (Groupe d'Étude et d'Information sur les Phénomènes Aérospatiaux Non-identifiés). Sightings reported to the French police are passed on to GEIPAN, which works with the French space agency (CNES) in Toulouse. Previously called GEPAN.

geoglyph (n.): A design carved into the ground and visible from the sky, such as the Nazca Lines. Larger and more permanent than crop circles*, these "geoglyphs" are often interpreted as coded messages directed at exocivilizations* or as UFO* runways.

Gray (n.): An alien with bluish-gray skin, whose body consists of two short legs, two long arms, and a disproportionately sized head with two generally downturned, almond-shaped eyes. An autopsy of the body found at Roswell, New Mexico, was said to be of a "Gray." Within this category, ufologists differentiate between extra-terrestrials of two different sizes, with "Little Grays" apparently being cloned copies of Grays.

Green Aliens (n.): Small extraterrestrials with viscous, greenish skin. Science fiction authors often saddle them with a visible brain, tentacu-lar limbs, and a glow-in-the-dark aura. Martians are often referred to as "little green men."

H̲

hybrid (n.): The result of a crossover between Grays* and humans, through biological contact or artificial insemination for eugenic purposes

I̲

implantee (n.): A human being abducted by aliens who then inserted an implant into their body, most often in the head. "Implantees" are hence "abductees" whom the EBE* want to keep controlling after their release.

intraterrestrial (adj. and n.): Related to Hollow Earth theories, the term refers to creatures inhabiting the inside of our planet. They would sometimes surface through airlocks or secret portals that are the source of legends about hell. According to Eastern traditions about the under-ground kingdom of Agartha, so-called Gypsies are said to be of "intraterrestrial" origin, which is how they received their knowledge of magic.

Invisible College (loc.): A secret international organization, consisting of public officials and high-level scientists for the study of UFOs*. The term "the College" is often employed without a descriptive adjective.

K̲

Koreshan (adj. and n.): Derived from the biblical name Koresh, equivalent to Cyrus and referring to a follower of a religion founded in 1869 by the American herbalist, alchemist, and visionary Cyrus Reed Teed (1829–1908), who had a woman appear to him in a dream revealing that all of humanity lived inside—not on the surface—of our planet.

L

Lizzy (n.): Derived from the word "lizard," this is a nickname for extraterrestrial Reptilians*.

M

MiB (abr.): Acronym for the US American designation "Men in Black," referring to secret service agents who investigate UFO* sightings and who are described by contactees* as men always dressed in black. In addition to just collecting data, they are also rumored to have committed various acts of intimidation and manipulation; see cover-up*, debunking*, MILABS*, etc.

MILABS (n., pl.): Military abduction whose victims include EBE* crashed on Earth, but also contactees* who are not careful enough or too talkative

missing time (loc.): This term refers to a period of time in which the contactees* and especially the abductees* have no memory, except for the implanted screen memories*.

MJ-12 (abr.): Referring to Majestic, the highest degree of confidentiality classification in the US army, this code name designates a supposedly clandestine organization that governs the US intelligence services. Indeed, conspiracy theorists assume that America's technological advances are based on extraterrestrial influences, which implies a secret government consisting of initiated members, and even the organized control of the country by infiltrated starseeds*.

N

Nordic (n.): A humanoid alien of the Scandinavian type. Synonymous with Blond* or Tall*.

P

pelicanist (adj. and n.): A skeptic who is forever seeking to explain aerial phenomena by using mundane facts, however unconvincing they may be. The word comes from the Mount Rainier case in 1947, when some commentators argued that Kenneth Arnold (1915–1984) had not come across flying saucers* but, in fact, a pod of pelicans.

Pleiadian (adj. and n.): An alien of the "sixth density" (i.e., immaterial), who communicates with earthlings by telepathy or channeling*. They are from the Pleiades, a star cluster in the constellation Taurus. According to the contactee* Barbara Marciniak, they are identical to the Arcturians* and the Cassiopeians*, and their immateriality allows them to emit signals using any kind of conducive airwaves.

posadist (adj. and n.): A supporter or disciple of the Argentine Trotskyist Homero Rómulo

Cristalli Frasnelli (1912–1981), known by his pseudonym Juan Posadas as the father of Marxist ufology*. According to activists of the Fourth International Posadist, aliens have moved beyond the class struggle to reach the stage of a communist society, giving them a technological advantage from which their backward earthling comrades will benefit. Some posadists go so far as to suggest that their leaders in the proletarian revolution were of extraterrestrial origin, such as Karl Marx (1818–1883).

R

Raëlist(adj. and n.): A disciple of Raël, also known as "the Messenger," whose real name was Claude Vorilhon. The former comedic singer and sports journalist is said to have seen a flying saucer* on a volcano in the Auvergne in 1973 and, in 1975, was apparently transported to the planet of the Elohim*, who introduced him to their secrets, making him the "prophet of the third millennium." He founded MADECH, the "Movement for the Welcoming of the Elohim*, Creators of Humanity" (Mouvement pour l'accueil des Elohims créateurs de l'humanite), which became the Raëlian movement.

Reptilian (n.): An alien with a reptile head and scales for skin. These hostile, malodorous, and probably carnivorous visitors to Earth are also called lizards* or Saurians* and apparently have their eye on world domination. Some ufologists* say about these beings that they can take on human form in the presence of earthlings, and argue that they have already taken control of important positions of power. Several monarchs in Europe, including Queen Elizabeth II of England, are apparently Reptilian infiltrators.

S

saucerian (adj.): A pejorative term to describe ufologists* and disciples of associated cults

Saurians (n.): A synonym for Reptilian*

scoop mark (loc.): A visible scar on the body of an abductee* that shows that the person has been subjected to surgical examinations

screen memories (loc.): False memories inserted in the memory of contactees* and especially abductees* to erase any memory of the experiences to which they have been subjected

Selenite (adj. and n.): In reference to the Greek goddess Selene, the term refers to a resident of the moon.

Sirian (adj. and n.): An alien originating from Sirius. The Dogon people of West Africa are said to have "Sirian" ancestry.

star child (loc.): Also called "star people," this term refers to a child who is the offspring of an earthling inseminated by an alien or member of another exocivilization*.

starseed (n.): Human being of extraterrestrial origin

Symmes hole (loc.): In reference to Captain John Cleves Symmes Jr. (1780–1829), one of the leading Hollow Earth theorists, these are presumed entrances to the core of the earth. Apparently there are several "Symmes holes" on the surface of planet Earth that allow intraterrestrials* to surface now and then. The two main holes are said to be located on the north and south poles.

T

tachyon (n.): A particle or wave whose velocity exceeds the speed of light, which suggests its negative mass and a reversal of the flow of time

tachyonic (adj.): Relating to tachyons*: some UFOs* are propelled by "tachyonic engines," drawing their energy from a nebulous "tachyonic field" with unlimited resources.

Tall (n.): A humanoid alien of the Scandinavian type. Synonymous with Blond* or Nordic*.

triangle (n.): A type of UFO* of triangular shape, rarely observed, except above Belgium in 1989

U

UAP (abr.): Stands for "unidentified aerial phenomenon," the official terminology used by the US authorities to refer to UFOs*

UFO (abr.): Also spelled "ufo," this common name is the acronym for "unidentified flying object." A definition by negatives identifies a UFO as an unexplained aerial phenomenon. Its extraterrestrial origin is only a hypothesis that ufologists* try to prove.

UFOish (adj.): Relating to UFOs* and ufology*

ufology (n.): Derived from the acronym "UFO" to refer to unidentified flying objects, the term describes the study of UFOs*.

ufologist (n.): A UFO specialist*, an author of articles or works on ufology*

ufonaut (n.): The pilot or passenger of an UFO*

Ummite (adj. and n.): Term relating to the mysterious exoplanet* Ummo, whose benevolent inhabitants have allegedly sent numerous written messages to several people on earth to encourage research and peace.

V

vortex (n.): A swirling movement produced by fluid matter or particles

W

wow (signal) (onom.): An extraterrestrial signal detected in the context of the SETI (Search for Extraterrestrial Intelligence) program

X

xenobiology (n.): The study of life forms of mysterious origin

Xipéhuz (n., pl.): Luminescent immaterial presences of various geometric shapes that appeared in London in 1887. They were the spearheads of the first science fiction novel, *The Xipéhuz*, by Rosny Aîne (1856–1940).

Z

Zeta Reticulan (adj. and n.): An extraterrestrial from Zeta Reticuli, a distant constellation from which the Grays* apparently originate

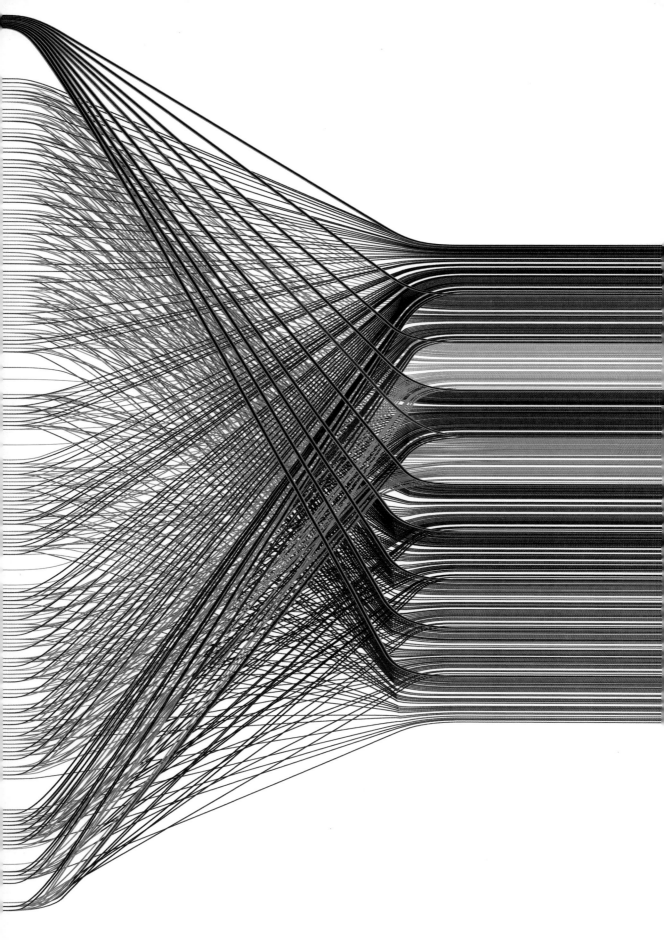

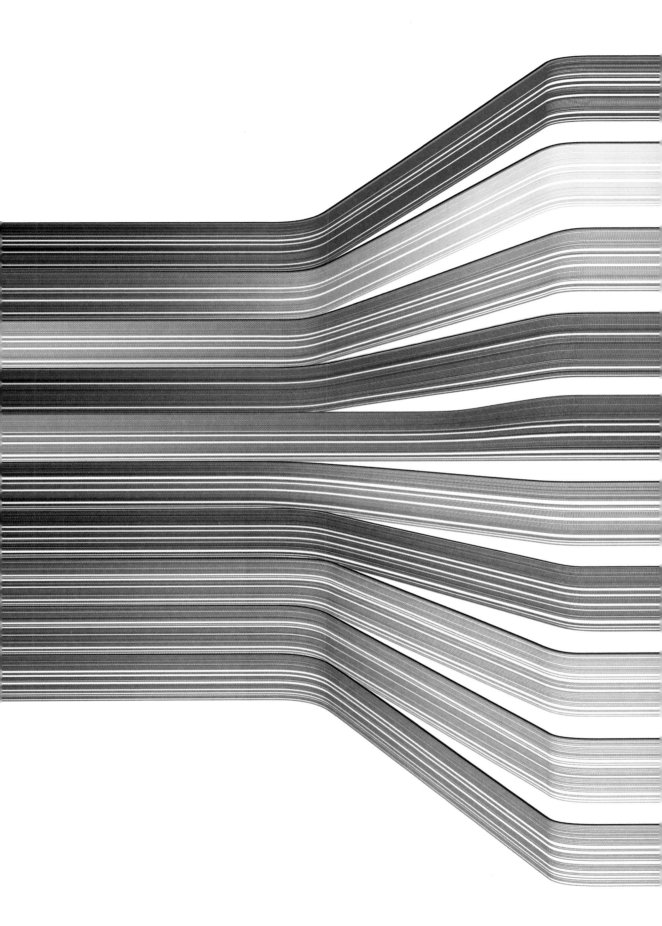

There is an infinite number of worlds.
Some like this world; others unlike it.

—Epicurus, *Letters to Herodotus*

We have here a golden opportunity of seeing how a legend is formed, and how in a difficult and dark time for humanity a miraculous tale grows up.

—Carl Jung, *Flying Saucers: A Modern Myth of Things Seen in the Skies*

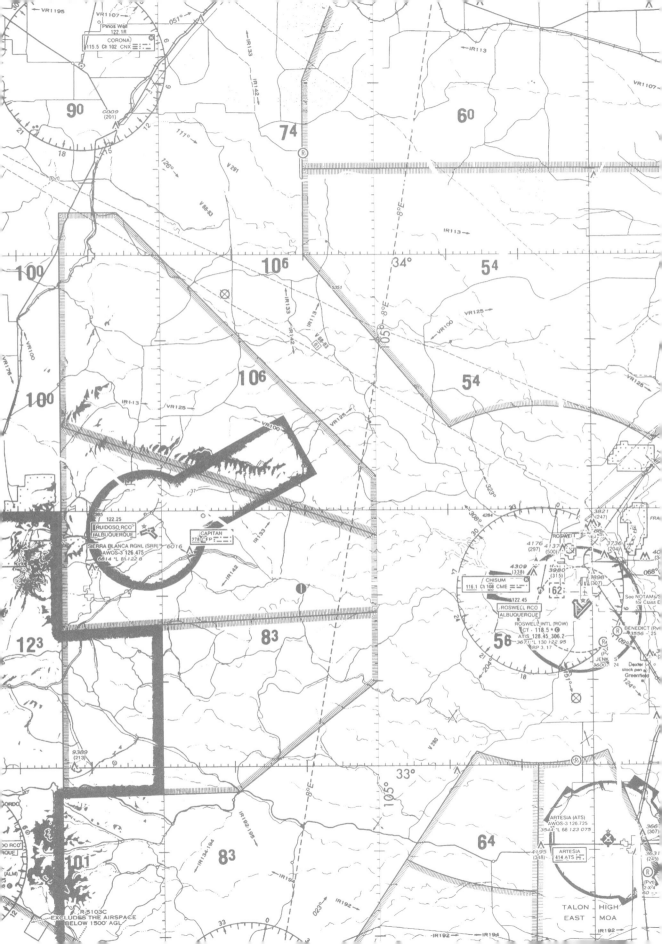

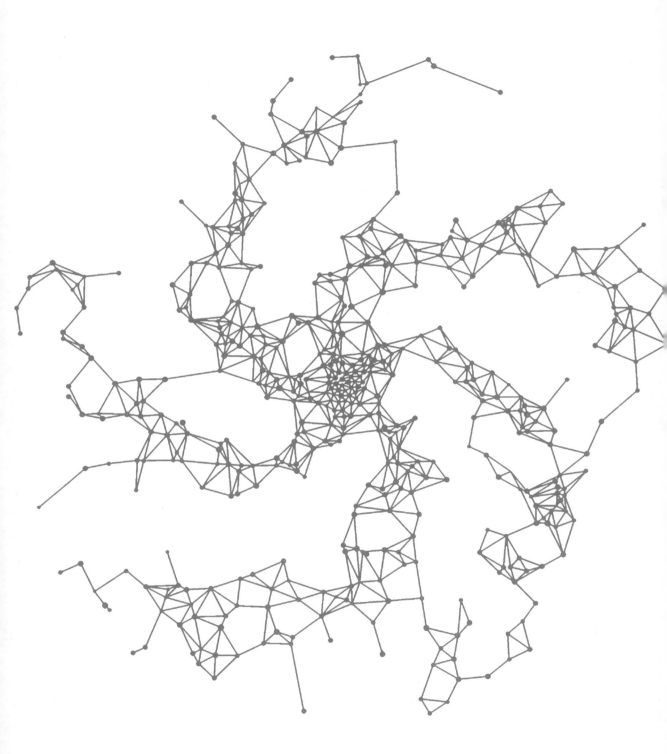

[I]f our solar system is not unusual, then there are so many planets in the universe that, for example, they outnumber the sum of all sounds and words ever uttered by every human who has ever lived. To declare that Earth must be the only planet with life in the universe would be inexcusably bigheaded of us.

—Neil DeGrasse Tyson, *Death by Black Hole*

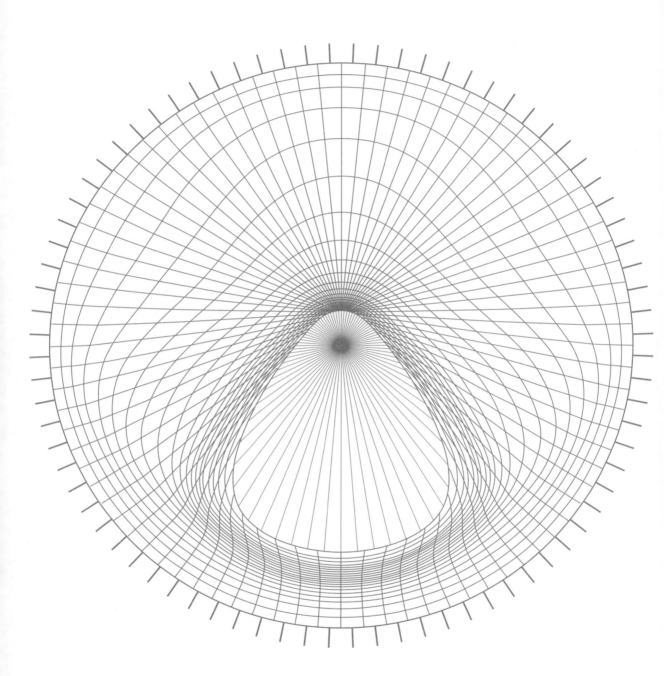

IN THE SAME SERIES

Atlas of Dream Lands

Atlas of Lost Paradises

Atlas of Seawrecks and Other Fortunes of the Sea

Atlas of Wild and Remote Lands

Atlas of Elementary Botany by Jean-Jacques Rousseau

Atlas of Cursed Places

Atlas of Lost cities